D0917060

ALSO *by* DAVID RITZ

BIOGRAPHIES:

Divided Soul: The Life of Marvin Gaye

Faith in Time: The Life of Jimmy Scott

AUTOBIOGRAPHIES:

Ray Charles: *Brother Ray*

Smokey Robinson: *Inside My Life*

B.B. King: *Blues All Around Me*

Etta James: *Rage to Survive*

The Neville Brothers: *The Brothers*

Jerry Wexler: *Rhythm & the Blues*

Aretha Franklin: *From These Roots*

Walter Yetnikoff: *Howling at the Moon*

Robert Guillaume: *Guillaume: A Life*

Laila Ali: *Reach*

Gary Sheffield: *Inside Power*

Felicia "Snoop" Pearson:
Grace After Midnight

Lang Lang: *Journey of a Thousand Miles*

Don Rickles: *Rickles' Book*

Don Rickles: *Rickles' Letters*

Leiber and Stoller: *Hound Dog*

Paul Shaffer: *We'll Be Here for the Rest of Our Lives*

Grandmaster Flash: *The Adventures of Grandmaster Flash: My Life, My Beats*

Tavis Smiley: *What I Know for Sure*

Cornel West: *Brother West*

Archbishop Carl Bean: *I Was Born This Way*

Natalie Cole: *Love Brought Me Back*

Janet Jackson: *True You*

NOVELS:

Search for Happiness

The Man Who Brought the Dodgers Back to Brooklyn

Blue Notes Under a Green Felt Hat

Barbells and Saxophones

Family Blood

Take It Off! Take It All Off!

Passion Flowers

Sanctified Blues
(cowritten with Mable John)

Stay Out of the Kitchen!
(cowritten with Mable John)

Love Tornado
(cowritten with Mable John)

INSPIRATIONAL:

Messengers: Portraits of African American Ministers, Evangelists, Gospel Singers, and Other Messengers of "the Word"

NOT DEAD &
NOT FOR SALE

THE EARTHLING PAPERS   A MEMOIR

SCOTT WEILAND

WITH DAVID RITZ

SCRIBNER

NEW YORK LONDON TORONTO SYDNEY

SCRIBNER
A Division of Simon & Schuster, Inc.
1230 Avenue of the Americas
New York, NY 10020

First Scribner hardcover edition May 2011

SCRIBNER and design are registered trademarks of The Gale Group, Inc.,
used under license by Simon & Schuster, Inc., the publisher of this work.

For information about special discounts for bulk purchases,
please contact Simon & Schuster Special Sales at 1-866-506-1949
or business@simonandschuster.com.

The Simon & Schuster Speakers Bureau can bring authors to your live event.
For more information or to book an event contact the Simon & Schuster
Speakers Bureau at 1-866-248-3049 or visit our website at www.simonspeakers.com.

Designed by Brian Chojnowski

Manufactured in the United States of America

10   9   8   7   6   5   4   3   2   1

Library of Congress Cataloging-in-Publication Data

Weiland, Scott.
Not dead & not for sale / Scott Weiland with David Ritz. —1st Scribner hardcover ed.
p.   cm.
1. Weiland, Scott, 1967– 2. Rock musicians—United States—Biography. 3.
Stone Temple Pilots (Musical group). I. Ritz, David. II. Title. III.
Title: Not dead and not for sale.
ML420.W357A3 2010
782.42166092—dc22   2010025147
[B]

ISBN 978-0-7432-9716-5
ISBN 978-1-4391-9997-8 (ebook)

*I dedicate this book
to my beautiful children,
Noah and Lucy*

NOT DEAD & NOT FOR SALE

The Earthling Papers

As a baby, I was a dead-ringer for my son, Noah. Here I am, already interested in music and, as you can see, a believer that one should own one's own albums.

PRELUDE *to the* PRELUDE

This memoir took me unknowingly to new highs and new and uncharted lows. It's been a pleasure to work with David Ritz, an artist and tireless worker. I've relived pains as well as the highest of heights. I've felt deflated and elated to dig through the maze that is the mind and soul. Mining through the cobwebs to explore the why's and why not's. The human heart filled with sorrows and gold inspired me to dig further through this marathon or labyrinth in order to get the answers, find truth, and forgive injustices endured in order to move forward happy mostly, sad lovingly, and purged of the nightmares of the past. It's been a grand endeavor. But worth it.

Peace to All,
Scott R. Weiland

I T'S 2010 AND IMPROBABLY—hell, impossibly—Stone Temple Pilots is back together and blazing hot, especially after our second single debuted at number one.

Our new single debuted at number one.

Our new album is selling like crazy.

Old fans are back. New fans are lining up. Even the critics, who once delighted in deflating us, are praising us to the sky.

We were written off as the band of disastrous dysfunction with too many personal problems to survive. Or rather, I was written off as the guy whose hopeless addictions had—and would always—ruin everything for everyone.

Well, here we are, like Led Zep, playing sold-out arenas all over the world.

I couldn't be happier.

And I couldn't be more pissed because one rock-and-roll rag, our nemesis from back in the day, has, like the monster from the black lagoon, reemerged. They did a profile of me that was so off I didn't even recognize myself. Quotes were taken out of context and old clichés about me were rewritten to look new.

Well, maybe the timing of this wrong-headed article isn't so bad after all. Maybe it serves to remind me how glad I am to be offering up my own story in my own words. As you'll see, I'm not afraid of documenting details about the life I've led. I have nothing to hide. I've done what I've done. I've done loads of things right and loads of things wrong that could be considered uncouth. It's all here, all documented in my dreams, my musical schemes, my drama-poem-lyrics.

You'll see that much of this has to do with love. I'm in love with love—or is it the idea of being in love with love? I believe that love only happens truly twice, but why, I wonder, does love always equal a broken heart?

With all this in mind, I've decided to tell my story. I've sold nearly 40 million records and at the time I didn't appreciate it much. I felt it would be different later with *Magnificent Bastards*, both solo records (*Twelve Bar Blues* and *Happy in Galoshes*), Velvet Revolver, and finally the rebirth of STP. This book is an attempt to appreciate the complexity of so much success in the midst of so much chaos.

I wrote these "Earthling Papers" so you can hear directly from me. I'm not arrogant enough to call it *the* truth. But I do call it *my* truth. My life had been twisted, demoralized, redemptive, remarkable.

Let me start by jumping back to the point, only two years ago, when my mind was a mess.

Be ready for the rabbit hole.

PRELUDE

EVERY TIME I TRY TO CATCH UP TO MY LIFE, something stops me. Different people making claims on my life. Old friends telling me new friends aren't true friends. All friends trying to convince me that I can't survive without them.

Then there are the pay-for-hire get-off-drugs professionals with their own methods and madness. They help, they hurt, they welcome me into their institutions . . . and, well, their madness.

Welcome to my life.

Two years ago, my life was self-restricted to a sober living house, meaning that I walked through the doors of my own free will. Within hours, I watched the game of communal free will get stepped on, laughed at, and batted around like a Ping-Pong ball.

One of my fellow patients was a rocker chick just turned twenty-one. She had a problem with depression. We met in the lounge and talked the night away, smoking cigarettes, exchanging words of comfort.

"Am I pretty?" she asked me.

"You are beautiful," I told her.

"Everyone says I smell because I haven't showered."

"Everyone can get fucked," I told her. "When you're depressed, you're not exactly in the mood for a shower."

She told me a story of grief and confusion. I listened. When she was through, we hugged good night. She kissed me sweetly. She wanted more.

"We can't do this," I said. "It's not right. Not now, not here."

A day later, I was approached by one of the counselors whom I considered a first-class shit talker.

"Rumor has it that the two of you were intimate."

"What's intimate?" I asked.

"Sex."

"No!"

"She obviously has a crush on you."

"Okay. What of it?"

"I heard you two had sex in the Jacuzzi."

"No Jacuzzi," I said. "No sex. Besides, who has sex in a Jacuzzi?"

"I want to know what happened," she insisted.

"We were flirtatious. That was inappropriate. So we stopped."

This young woman was confronted at our next group session. Sixteen hours later, she sliced her leg down past the fatty tissue. She was a cutter. They took her out of the villa and put her in a psych ward.

What can I do about it?

I write a poem, "The Little Villa and Painted Egg."

Minds squall, alcohol, heroin
The man, the boy, the girl
The little villa where you live
You need to fill that pain inside
Xanex, Valium, barbiturates—they ease the easy side
Of all you fucked-up managerial types

_____

You love to rule by what you say
Not by what you find
Beautiful garden, Easter eggs, those that you never really had
You stole our experiences and stole our baskets
That's how you found twenty-one out of fifty-seven

THAT WAS LAST MONTH. This week I'm home dealing with those who "manage" my business life, those who, for their own purposes, direct my moves. They are my partners, assistants, and drug coaches (whom we call "minders"). There is no peace, not for an hour, not for thirty seconds. Someone is always showing up with calculated suggestions and implied instructions. I don't know, but I think I've done pretty well for myself, even during my long-lasting, narcotic misadventures—all without the protective bubble of paranoid employees, partners, and helpers—er, minders.

Meanwhile, the facts are these:

It has been eight and a half years since I shot dope and nearly three years since I did coke.

I still drink. A regular garden-variety boozer, I am like any other barfly or drink-alone kind of guy. My relationship to liquor is not romantic the way I once envisioned my love affair with dope. I struggle to stop drinking, but I don't see it as suicidal. In any event, I'm not drinking today. Today I'm inviting you into the middle of my life and the middle of my head. My heart feels a bit closed off because I'm realizing that there are few people, if any, that I fully trust. That's an amazing statement to make and brings me to what may be the purpose of this book.

How did I get to this point? One word could probably suffice—*loss.*
I'm searching for explanations.

_____

Someone recently gave me a T-shirt that said, I'M IN LIKE SEVEN BANDS.

There is a Stone Temple Pilots story to tell. There is a Velvet Revolver story to tell. There is a love story to tell. And a drug story to tell.

AMONG MY GREAT LOVES is that category of substances called heroin. Narcotic alkaloids. Derivatives of opium. I describe this stuff lovingly. I do so at the risk of high irresponsibility. It is not my intention to mislead anyone looking to live a righteous life. God knows that the shit will kill you, inside and out, soul to the bone. At the same time, I am committed to an honest assessment of the wreckage of my past. I loved opiates; I hated opiates; I am attracted to opiates perhaps the way John Keats was attracted to death. One hundred ninety years ago, the romantic poet wrote "Ode to a Nightingale":

> I have been half in love with easeful Death,
> Call'd him soft names in many a mused rhyme,
> To take into the air my quiet breath;
> Now more than ever seems it rich to die,
> To cease upon the midnight with no pain,
> With thou art pouring forth thy soul abroad
> In such an ecstasy!

IS DEATH THE MUSE? Is rock and roll the nightingale? Are opiates the key to unlocking the magical kingdom where colorful flowers fade to black? Why should anyone—especially a kid or a man who suspects that he or she may have talent—be drawn to such a kingdom?

I don't know. Except that the pull is visceral. It may also be an act of self-loating or anger against home or society or even the human condition in which the promise of death shadows us from those first fresh moments of birth.

I think of the young woman overwhelmed by a compulsion to cut herself. The compulsion is heartbreaking and bizarre, but maybe not bizarre at all—maybe it's simply the most honest compulsion of all because it gets to the heart of the matter. My long opiate-dazed days and sleepless nights were all about cutting myself emotionally. When I got high, the last thing in the world I wanted to do was party or interact with other human beings. I retreated to the dark corners of my room and my life. I stayed alone and disappeared down black holes where no one could find me. I couldn't find myself. I didn't want to find myself. I became invisible. Or, as I put it in the song "Dead and Bloated," "I am smellin' like the rose that someone gave me on my birthday deathbed."

*Dad Kent and me
at age five*

*Dad Dave and me
at age three*

A

TALE

of

TWO

FATHERS

W HY IS THE WORLD SO DIFFERENT NOW? I used to take my fishing rod and go down to the lake by myself. Now the world is one organized playdate after another.

In my childhood, I relied on my imagination—I could walk in the woods and be in Camelot, or Narnia, or wherever my mind envisioned. I had a vivid imagination, and still do. Today, though, how can you compete with a computer that, with the touch of a button, gives you every answer to every question?

In a technologically more innocent era, I was born Scott Kline in Santa Cruz, California, on October 27, 1967, to Sharon and Kent Kline, who divorced when I was two. Then Mom married Dave Weiland and I became Scott Weiland. I lost my name. I lost my father. I gained another father. Later I resented the hell out of my blood father, Kent, for not insisting that I keep his name. I felt abandoned. *Gave his name away, gave his son away.* Meanwhile, I saw Kent as a cool dude who drove a Pepsi truck for a living but smoked dope at night and listened to the Doors and Merle Haggard. When I think about my dad and Martha, the artist he married after Mom, I hear Fleetwood Mac's *Rumours*. Kent's the father I wanted to be with. At age forty-two, I'm still looking to connect with him.

My new dad was a good guy whose middle name was discipline. An aeronautics engineer with TRW Space and Electronics, he was always working on advanced degrees. Shortly after he married Mom, he moved us to Chagrin Hills, a woodsy suburb outside Cleveland, Ohio.

I'm stuck on that name—*Chagrin Hills. Chagrin* means distress, pain, anxiety, sorrow, affliction, mental suffering. Usually, idyllic suburbs have names like Pleasant Valley or Paradise Falls. Chagrin Falls makes no sense. In some ways, my childhood made good sense; in other ways, it didn't.

My childhood was green pastures and bee stings, learning to play baseball and football, living in a nice house, waiting—always waiting— for the start of summer so I could go to California and see my dad Kent.

I was already a teenager when this dream started recurring. Its form changed slightly, but the basic structure stayed the same:

Posters are plastered all over the city—on billboards and buses, in splashy newspaper ads and screaming TV commercials. It's all over the radio and the Internet. It's tonight, it's now, it's what the world's been waiting for.

It's the ultimate Battle of the Bands.

Midnight tonight at a great outdoor stadium. The witching hour. The dark night of the soul. The moment of truth.

It's three years before I'm born.

Or maybe it's the year of my birth, or the moment of my birth.

Or maybe I'm three years old. Or five. Or ten.

Whatever my age, I'm there. I'm involved. I'm engaged. I'm riveted by the battle. My life is at stake.

My pulse is racing, my heart pounding inside my chest. The excitement has me crazy with anticipation.

—————

Two bands. Two bandstands.

The Rolling Stones versus the Kingston Trio.

Over the Stones flies a pirate flag. Over the Kingston Trio flies the stars and stripes.

Chaos versus Order.

Nihilism versus Responsibility.

Crooked versus Straight.

The crowd fills the stands.

Half of them are fraternity boys and sorority girls, suits and dresses, blazers and loafers. The other half are freaks, punks, dopers, bikers, renegades.

I'm sitting in the dugout next to my mom.

My father is introducing the Stones. He and Keith are dressed identically in psychedelic bell-bottoms. He and Mick are sharing a joint. He calls the Stones "the greatest rock-and-roll band in the world."

My stepdad introduces the Kingston Trio. They're all wearing button-down blue oxford shirts and neatly pressed khaki trousers. My stepdad says, "This is real music. This is harmony. This is beauty."

My father shouts over to him, "This is darkness! This is the real shit!"

"Go out there," my mom whispers in my ear. "Go out there and help."

I run out onto the field. I look up and see a hundred thousand screaming people. The bands have started playing simultaneously. Riffs of "Satisfaction." Riffs of "Tom Dooley." I run toward my dad, Kent, but he's disappeared into the crowd. Mick and Keith don't know me. Security is chasing after me. I'm chasing after my dad, but I can't find him. I'm running up and down, running all over the stadium, but I can't find him, can't find him, crying hysterically, I can't find my dad . . .

FATHERS AND SONS, SONS AND BROTHERS.

My brother, Michael, was born to my stepfather and my mother when I was four and a half. On the day Mom came home from the hospital, I remember bright sunshine lighting our house. When I saw my baby brother, I was filled with wonder. He was fast asleep; he looked helpless, adorable, more doll-like than human. Whenever he squeezed my finger with his tiny hand, I felt flooded with love. I wouldn't feel that kind of pure love until the birth of my own children. For the first time in my life, instead of worrying about being protected, I had someone to protect.

Me and Michael

The Scott-and-Michael story centers on two brothers to whom God gave musical talent. I'm the one who sought success; he's the one who feared it. We both fell into drink and drugs. When I got caught with a beer, our stepdad brought the wrath of the gods down on my head. When Michael got caught with pot, he said, "It's God's herb," and Father Dave just sort of shook his head. Maybe the wrath did me good. Maybe the tolerance did Michael harm. Later, I gave Michael his first beer, his first shot of dope, his first hit of crack. Do I feel guilty about that? Yes and no. I wish I hadn't made those introductions, but knowing Michael, he would have done anything anyway—just to get away. Michael was always way ahead of the curve.

Camping—hippy-style—a little weed and Big Foot: me at age six, cousin Chris, and Craig, 1973

In the lane the snow is glistening: my childhood house in Cleveland

A
TALE
of
TWO
STATES

T WO STATES OF MIND: Ohio and California. Ohio is cold and square; California is cool and hip. At least in the mind of a kid.

THE BEER BUZZ IS A SMALL BUZZ, but it's an intriguing buzz if you're looking for any kind of buzz. In the sixth grade, living in Cleveland, I lived for the summertime. Summertime meant California and my dad, Kent, and his wife, Martha. Summertime meant watching them cultivate their pot plants in the backyard and throwing their parties with Emmylou Harris and Stones records and margaritas and shots of Cuervo Gold. Summertime meant pals like Billy, a cool dude who already had long hair, Levi's super-bell cords, and Vans slip-ons. Billy was the first guy I met who played guitar. He taught himself Zeppelin and taught me about a beer buzz. Billy, my stepbrother, Craig, and Jonathan, the son of Martha's best friend, snuck beers out of Dad's fridge. While the grown-up party was building its own buzz, we chugged down the STONES RECORDS AND MARGARITAS AND SHOTS OF CUERVO GOLD brews, and then another, and another, and walked out into the backyard, the secret inside our heads. I liked the feeling of entering an alternate energy field. I liked the psychological and chemical rearrangement brought on by the alcohol.

Other times we invaded Dad's liquor cabinets: times when Billy, Craig, Jonathan, and I got sick, times when we pushed the envelope and smoked weed, which hit me like acid. I tripped on the sunlight streaming through a trellis fence. The pattern of shade became a three-dimensional revelation, a maze containing the very mystery of life, a key connecting all feelings to all forms.

Back in Cleveland for the seventh grade, the California sunshine was replaced with the Ohio snow. My Ohio friends weren't as cool as Billy. My Ohio extracurricular activities centered on sports. Breaking tackles. Wrestling and fishing. Getting up at six a.m. in the dark for swimming practice and going at it again after school.

One day I came home from school and walked over to my friend Mark's house. His parents, who worked late, had a killer liquor cabinet. Over ice, I filled a tumbler with Black Velvet, gin, and vodka, took it to the woods, sat against a tree, and drank it down. The moment was pivotal precisely because it was solitary. I got blasted all alone. The isolation did something to me—removed me from life and reality—that I experienced as strangely wonderful.

The winter was long. I studied the calendar, watching the months slowly pass until fall gave way to winter, winter to spring, and spring to summertime back in California, where I learned to surf. I wasn't a champ, but I could do it. While surfing I felt free from time, suspended in space, thoughtless and alive.

———————

HAVING TWO DADS AND NO DAD WAS CONFUSING. I wanted my biological dad but he seemed to want me only during the summers. He was the one listening to Hank Williams. My stepdad was telling me to do my homework. Meanwhile, the teachers told my stepdad that I was smart but hyper. I was diagnosed with attention deficit disorder. Psychologists suggested that I go on Ritalin. Mom wouldn't allow it. But she would allow me to visit her ex-husband at the end of the school year. So I was off to California to visit Dad and Martha and Martha's son, Craig, who was my age. Craig was a great guy and one of my closest friends, but I couldn't help but be a little jealous of him. He had my dad's attention all the time. Craig had become my replacement. Then two years later, Craig was dead.

Me hugging Craig

I REMEMBER SITTING IN MR. BURKE'S creative-writing class. Mr. Burke was my favorite teacher. The school year was almost over. I was still in shock. I still couldn't process the news. Mr. Burke knew what happened back in California. He told me to write about it. He said writing would help. I remembered then—and still remember now—every moment, every conversation that took place between me and Craig. Our encounters were etched into my psyche.

I wrote this:

"Yesterday was rainy. The sky was crying rain. I was standing at the end of our driveway when I heard my mother's voice. She said, 'Hurry, Scott, there's a call for you.' I ran in the house. My heart was beating like crazy. I knew something was wrong. My father's voice sounded different. His voice was crying pain."

From there, I wrote another ten pages, raw words flowing out of the ink like a bad, black dream.

I turned in the paper and the teacher understood. That's all I could write. I'd memorized my father's words, but couldn't repeat them: "Craig was riding a wheelie. You know how he's the best wheelie rider around. He didn't see the car coming. It hit him head-on. His brain is swelling. There's a hole in his brain. They're operating tonight." I couldn't repeat what my father said when he called the next morning: "Craig's dead." I couldn't describe my memories of how, for week after week, month after month, year after year, Dad would take me and Craig dirt-bike riding.

I couldn't say anything when I visited Dad that summer. He was completely remote and removed from me. I couldn't tell him—couldn't tell anyone—about the feelings overwhelming me. I was angry, guilty, sad, resentful, longing to have my father back. I was covered with confusion.

———————

FATHERS AND SONS, SONS AND BROTHERS.

Craig was my brother, and even though he wasn't Dad's blood son, I know that when Craig died, part of Dad died with him. That's a part of my father I've never been able to reach. Much later in life when my brother Michael died, part of me disappeared and has never returned. It hurts to love.

Leaping for the stars

"TRIPPIN'

as I'M

THINKIN'"

—*from "Crackerman"*

N O ONE TURNS YOU INTO A DRUG ADDICT OR DRUNK. The blame game is pointless and harmful. I don't believe in pointing fingers. We do what we do and are responsible for our own actions. I don't believe we are victimized by circumstance. There are, however, stories to be told. The story does not begin with us, but rather our parents, and our parents' parents. The story goes back further than we know or can even imagine. Our stories are linked together because we share this space on the planet. We influence one another, whether we like it or not.

I love my mother. Without doubt she's been my biggest supporter—true, loving, and loyal. She's an independent woman who has always held down well-paying professional jobs. She's smart, understanding, and kind. She's also identified herself as an alcoholic.

When I was a preteen and still living in Cleveland, my stepfather took our family to a Cavaliers basketball game. We sat in the private box owned by TRW, his employer, that had leather seats and a fully stocked bar. After the game was over, Dave went into my mother's purse to look for something. He discovered a bottle of vodka that Mom was stealing from the bar. That's how she was busted.

———————

She had hit bottom—or enough of a bottom for her to feel remorse and respond honestly. She admitted her problem. In front of Dave, me, and Michael, she started crying. She said she was a loser. We cried even louder and said, "Mom, you're not a loser. We love you."

At the time, I didn't know the meaning of alcoholism. All I knew was that Mom was calling herself a horrible mother, and I knew that wasn't true. I knew she cared for us deeply. I watched her join a twelve-step program that she followed diligently. She didn't drink for some twenty-five years, and only started again after she learned that both her sons were heroin users. She slipped, as I have slipped, as I come from a long line of slippers. My uncle—Mom's brother—was an alcoholic and coke addict. My grandparents—Mom's mother and father—were hard-core alcoholics. Booze runs wild in my family.

JERRY JEFF WALKER SANG A SONG called "Jaded Lover." I heard it for the first time during one of those summers that I spent with my biological father, Kent. Dad could sing like Jerry Jeff; he could also sound like George Strait. His voice was resonant and deep and full of warmth. In a strange way, when I listened to the lyrics of "Jaded Lover"—"Well, it won't be but a week or two . . . you'll be out lovin' someone new"—I thought of the troubled relationship between me and Dad.

I felt like the jaded lover, the son he gave up, the son he could never quite embrace, the son who wanted the father more than the father wanted the son.

MY EARLIEST SEXUAL EXPERIENCES WERE NOT JOYFUL. When I was twelve and still living in Ohio, some girls invited me to play truth or dare.

We went to a barn with a haystack, the perfect setting. Little by little, we dared each other to undress. The Southern Comfort we were drinking out of a mason jar bolstered our courage. The game was going well when suddenly a big muscular guy, a high school senior, showed up and decided to fuck one of the girls in full view of all of us. The girl was willing but the party was ruined. None of us wanted to be there.

Turned out that the same dude rode the bus with me every day to school. One day he invited me to his house. This is a memory I suppressed until only a few years ago when, in rehab, it came flooding back. Therapy will do that to you.

The dude raped me.

It was quick, not pleasant. I was too scared to tell anyone.

"Tell anyone," he warned, "and you'll never have another friend in this school. I'll ruin your fuckin' reputation."

What do you do with that fear? That pain? How do memories get suppressed, and where do they go to hide?

INNOCENCE VERSUS CORRUPTION.

Hope versus despair.

I had the hope that comes with being a kid with natural athletic ability. In baseball, I had only one pitch—a fastball—but hardly anyone could hit it. By the eighth grade, I was able to launch a football fifty yards. The summer before my freshman year, I practiced with the team every day and achieved my goal: I was tapped as starting quarterback.

I was haunted by a dream that, decades later, still recurs:

I'm in the huddle, call the play, get the snap, drop back to pass, survey the field, and see, thirty yards away, my wide receiver two steps ahead of his defender. I cock my arm, and, just when I'm ready to launch a rocket, the football slips out of my hand for no reason. A lineman recovers the fumble and the game is lost.

Despite some obvious fears, I was a good athlete. I had a certain wholesome outlook on life. Look at the posters in my room: the famous

What everyone wanted for me

Farrah Fawcett bathing-suit pose, pictures of badass boxers like Marvelous Marvin Hagler, Sugar Ray Leonard, and Thomas "Hitman" Hearns. I was the All-American Ohio boy with a far-off dream of playing for Notre Dame, just as Dad Dave had done.

I wanted the prestige and attention that came with being QB—not to mention the thrill that comes with being the field general. I thrived on competition.

When it came to music, I also had a California-Ohio hip-square split. My first LPs were *The Captain and Tennille's Greatest Hits* and Elton John's *Captain Fantastic and the Brown Dirt Cowboy*. I was unapologetic in my passion for Tennille's version of "Love Will Keep Us Together," one of Neil Sedaka's best songs. In Ohio, my mother developed a love for John Denver's music that, according to her former husband's new wife, Martha, was a sign of squareness. As a member in good standing of the square Cleveland burbs, I joined the school choir. Riding in the back of my parents' Cadillac, I listened to *Peter and the Wolf* by Sergei Prokofiev, visualizing the animals depicted by the clarinet, oboe, horns, and bassoon.

I got religion.

I would wander over to Chagrin Falls Parks. The people who lived there, almost exclusively black, called it "The Park." I liked that neighborhood and, in fact, in the sixth grade I had a crush on a beautiful black girl.

In my preteen years, I had developed a deep and abiding love of God, inspired by the ministry of Father Plato and Father Trevisin. Dave brought us into the Catholic fold. My mother had been Episcopalian but felt comforted by the progressive view of Christ afforded by these two gentle priests. It wasn't about fire and brimstone, guilt or punishment. It was about a compassionate and patient love that doesn't judge, scorn,

_____

or scold. "Be not afraid. I go before you always. Come follow me and I will give you rest." I related to the notion of a mystic, all-accepting, all-forgiving love. I wanted it.

I became an altar boy. I wore the robes. During Mass, I brought the wine and the host to the priests. I lit the candles. Today, no matter where I am—tour bus, hotel room, studio, cabin in the woods—I light the candles. They calm me, center me, remind me of a time when God sat in the center of my heart. Not that He's ever disappeared. The candles bring Him back. I need to light them, every day and every night.

I WAS BURNING BRIGHTLY IN CLEVELAND. As a freshman, my first game at quarterback was only weeks away. I couldn't wait. I smelled triumph; I longed for glory. And then, just like that, Dave made the announcement: I wouldn't be playing the game; I wouldn't even be going to that school. I'd be leaving my best friend, Rich Remias, who came over practically every night to play Dungeons & Dragons. Like me, Rich came from a broken home; he understood me. It hurt to leave Rich, but there was nothing I could do. We were moving, and we were leaving immediately. We were winging our way back to California. I didn't know what to think. Didn't know what to feel. I was fourteen.

Senior class picture. Ahh, such a nice kid. Too bad in three years I'd be a strung-out junkie.

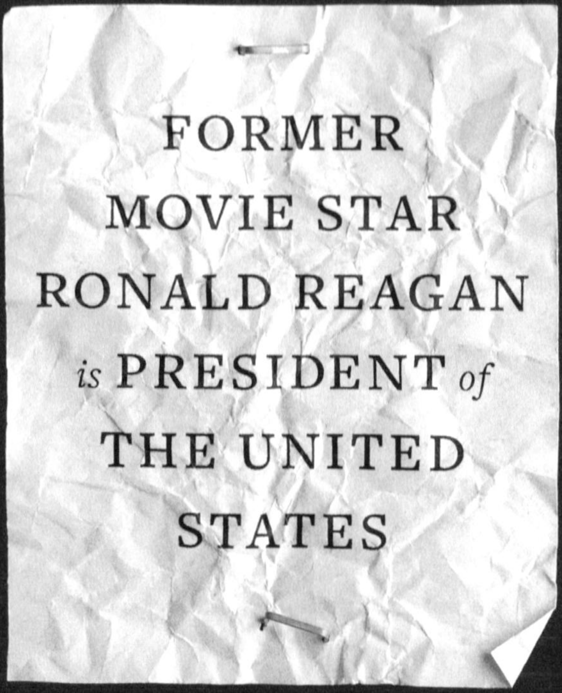

FORMER
MOVIE STAR
RONALD REAGAN
is PRESIDENT *of*
THE UNITED
STATES

1982.

Orange County, bastion of reactionary Republicanism but also stronghold of punk-rock counterculture.

Our house was three blocks from the beach and directly across from Edison High, scene of my new life.

First thing I did was hand a note to the football coach. It was a message from my old coach that said I was a starting QB. The new coach wasn't overly impressed. I was five eleven and weighed 155 pounds. The Edison team had won several championships. I'd have to wait.

By sophomore year I was one of the rotating quarterbacks. I also played defense. Going for an interception, I was speared from behind and knocked out of commission for a couple of weeks. I took that time to consider the options. I could keep playing, but without much of a chance to start at QB because, I always thought, my parents weren't doling out money to the boosters' club, or I could try something else. Rock-and-roll, like a siren song, was calling to me.

   I met Cory Hickok on the football team. He played tight end but, more important, he played guitar in his big brother's punk band, Awkward Positions. Cory turned me on to punk. In Ohio, I knew about Devo. I had listened to the Sex Pistols, whose *Never Mind the Bollocks* was our generation's *Exile on Main Street*. But Cory played me the Clash. He played me Sweet. He introduced me to Echo and the Bunnymen. I can't tell you how many times we listened to Queen's *Sheer Heart Attack*, a cool power-pop-punk hybrid. Cory had great ears and great taste.

He was over six feet and bone thin. Cool and quiet. A true-blue dude, he was a loving guy from a Christian family. Because my folks trusted his parents, I'd tell them I was staying at Cory's whenever I went out to party. Cory was also a good artist. I admired his drawings and how he looked at life artistically. I had other hipster friends on the football team like Rich Smith, the guy who helped me upgrade my surfing and scamming skills. Rich was the first guy I heard refer to girls as "birds" and "chicks."

HARD-CORE POSTPUNK BIG-BEAT GARAGE BANDS

AT SCHOOL, I WAS ACTIVE IN THE CHOIR AND SPORTS—wrestling, volleyball, soccer, football. My stepdad, diligently working till all hours, never attended my football games. Meanwhile, I was attracted to a flourishing alternative-music scene. Shaped by the sounds of Social Distortion, hard-core postpunk big-beat garage bands were popping up everywhere. But I was not impressed with what I heard in the local clubs. I thought I could do better. I formed a postpunk band.

AUGUST 1987
$1.95

GIG
MAGAZINE

BULK RATE
U.S. Postage
PAID
Northridge, CA
Permit No. 192

P.O. Box 7335
Northridge, CA 91327-7335

Improving
Your Vocals —
Both Onstage & Off

Tips & Techniques for:
- Guitarists
- Keyboardists
- Drummers
- Working Bands!

Home Recording Workshop
Win Two Audix Microphones!
Solutions Through Signal Process

ON THE COVER

The band Soi Disant, based out of Huntington Beach, CA, has been gigging in and around the Los Angeles area for about two years. Composed of lead vocalist Scott Weiland, bassist Scott Tubbs, guitarist Corey Hickok, keyboardist Britton Willits and drummer Lonnie Tubbs, the french band name means "self style." And the group feels its music is very much that way.

The strictly originals band is currently receiving major label attention and will be showcasing for Triad Artists Management at the end of July. Says vocalist Weiland, "A lot of bands are writing about social problems, we write more on a personal level."

WHAT the FUCK DOES "SOI-DISANT" MEAN?

(We really never knew.
Fuck art, let's fart.)

EVERY BAND HAS A STORY. The Stones stayed together. The Beatles broke up. When Jim Morrison died, the Doors were never the same. When Kurt Cobain died, Nirvana died.

I believe most bands are born at a time of youthful optimism and fresh energy. The motivation is strong and the future unlimited. Why not think big? Why not live in hope rather than fear?

I wasn't fearful at Edison High when we began a band called Soi-Disant. The question we got over and over again was, "What the fuck does it mean?" The answer we gave was that in French it means something like "self-style" or "style of one's own." An artsy-fartsy French name perfectly fit our vision of an edgy postpunk band. The more obscure the name, the better. We were modeling ourselves after the first Duran Duran album and bands like Ultravox, the Cure, and U2. Combining that vibe with a dirty rocking punky backbeat, I wrote stories focusing on teen angst. None of us were exceptional, but we were okay. It was me singing, Cory on guitar, bassists Dave Stokes at one point, Scott Tubbs at another, Britt Willets on keys.

It had all started with a simple conversation between me and Cory. I'd been singing in the choir.

"You think you can sing in a rock band?" Cory asked.

"Sure," I said.

"I don't mean sing with your choir voice. I mean sing in a rock voice."

"Sure," I repeated.

I have a chameleon-like ability to sing in any style. As a singer, I've always had confidence. I spent lots of time listening to Bowie and John Lennon, models for using your voice like an instrument.

After a few months of playing, we cut a demo at a sixteen-track studio with a great name: *Gofer Baroque.* Turned out good. I saw that I could lay down distinct harmony parts and build up a layered vocal. I felt like a professional beginner.

Over the next few years, I'd slip into the Orange County alt scene, where I'd find great musical and chemical stimulation. It was a lot better than backyard beer bashes. There was a famous club called the Cuckoo's Nest that featured bands like Social Distortion and the Bell Jar. That's where I heard the astounding English guitarist Adam Elesh, who lived in Newport Beach. I remember getting stoned and watching Adam play along with a Pink Floyd record, re-creating David Gilmour's solos note for note. I'd never seen anyone manipulate effect pedals so deftly.

"How'd you get so good?" I asked him.

"I learned everything I could. And then I promptly forgot everything I learned and started over."

At a critical juncture, Adam gave us a strong taste of big-time rock-and-roll virtuosity. Soi-Disant had a regular gig in Newport Beach at Déjà Vu.

Pretentious-named rock band meets pretentious-named club.

We got two hundred dollars a night plus all the booze we could keep down. It was the summer before my junior year, a golden time, the ultra-eighties, the season of experimentation. We had progressed past practicing in my garage to rehearsing in the studio of Scott Tubbs, our bassist. Scott had been in the choir with me—actually the Madrigal Ensemble—where every Christmas we went caroling on Balboa Island with a group of "choir mice," our term for the straitlaced singers. One December we got everyone drunk on peppermint schnapps and, as a result, were kicked out of the ensemble.

The two Scotts spelled trouble. During one rehearsal, a trio of computer nerds showed up. Looking to ingratiate themselves with cool rockers, they offered us blow. Bring it on. One of the boys railed out a fat line seven inches long. I snorted it up and never felt better. "Want another?" he asked. "Yes," I answered. Line two sent me from Venus to Mars. The substance was flaky and just the slightest bit oily. It looked like abalone shell. Turned out the boys were dealing it and asked if we'd be interested in doing the same. My thought was, *Yes, this is the way to snort for free and feel good all the time.* One problem, though: I was broke. "No problem," said the nerd. "I'll front you." Fine, except that I never sold an ounce. I snorted up everything in my possession except for a small amount that my stepdad would find in my room. That small amount, you will soon see, led to a major crisis.

DAD DAVE HAD HIS POSITION AT TRW. Mom was selling real estate in Orange County. I was finding my way through society at Edison High, athletics, music, and girls. One girl, with whom I was sexual, became pregnant.

"I'm going to have an abortion," is all she said.

I didn't argue. I believed—and still do—that a woman has jurisdiction over her own body. But I was also heartbroken. I drove her to the clinic, and then I drove her home. Neither of us said a word. It was incredibly sad. We cried silently. Our relationship was ruined. Intimacy between us was no longer possible. The fun, the playfulness, the pleasure of sex was gone. Something tragic had happened.

The
TALE
of the
PORK
CHOP

T HE START OF MY FIRST GOLDEN LOVE AFFAIR. Heather.

"Affair" is the wrong word. "Affair" sounds sleazy. Heather was heavenly. Heather was true love. Heather was my soul, my future. When we met in high school, I was convinced that we would live happily ever after. There was her physical lure: lustrous, wavy brown hair; enticing heart-shaped buttocks; beautiful, big sky-blue eyes; full breasts; warm and loving smile. Then there was her metaphysical lure: She exuded sweetness and light; her temperament was soft and mellow; her kindness gentle as a summer breeze. Together, we could talk about anything. I knew that the love we made was enduring. It was a world away from casual puppy love; it existed in a far deeper dimension than your routine high school crush. It was, in short, forever.

One summer afternoon when we were sixteen, we were making sweet love in my bedroom when, like a bat out of hell, Dad Dave barged in. Enraged, he started screaming. We scrambled for our clothes. Heather rushed out of the house. I heard my stepdad calling her parents, explaining what happened. I was incensed. Coitus interruptus is one thing. Getting ratted out by Dad is another.

A postpunk song called "Pork Chop," sung in the mode of Echo and the Bunnymen, was playing inside my head. The chorus went, "Pork chop, pork chop, you better eat your pork chop."

That night at dinner, my stepdad was still furious.

"Aren't you going to eat that pork chop?" he asked.

"I already ate a pork chop," I said. "There were two. Now there's only one."

"PORK CHOP, PORK CHOP, YOU BETTER EAT YOUR

"There were never two," he insisted. "You need to eat that pork chop."

"I've already eaten a pork chop."

The music got louder: "Pork chop, pork chop, you better eat your pork chop."

His voice got louder. "Eat it!"

My voice got louder. "No!"

"You never ate a pork chop!"

"I did eat a pork chop!"

"Pork chop, pork chop, you better eat your pork chop."

"You must be on coke," he said. "You must be hallucinating."

"If I were on coke," I said, "I wouldn't be hallucinating. That would be acid."

My stepdad, six five and 240 pounds, exploded; he turned over the table and went after me with a clenched fist.

"Pork chop, pork chop, you better eat your pork chop."

He chased me around the kitchen but couldn't catch me. I ran up to my bedroom, locked the door, threw some clothes into a gym bag, climbed

PORK CHOP"

out the window, jumped onto the garage roof, jumped down onto the driveway, climbed on my bike, and took off. I went to a friend's house, where we got high and listened to records for five straight days.

Meanwhile, back at my parents' house, Dad Dave searched my bedroom and found weed and a little blow. Without telling me, they called the authorities. The first time I learned of their call, I was back at school. I was in music theory class. Our teacher was Mr. Otey who, at six foot four, was an imposing presence. I was also in the choir and band, but, because I wanted to learn more, I signed up for theory. The class wasn't all that stimulating. My mood was somewhere between anxious and bored.

On this particular morning, the room was eerily quiet as two policemen and two paramedics walked in. The paramedics were carrying a gurney. I overheard them say my name. Mr. Otey called me to the front of the room. The cops looked at me and said, "You got to come with us." My heart beat like crazy. The room got even quieter. I had no idea what the hell was happening. I couldn't think of what to do except follow orders. I had to follow them outside. It felt like every single student in school had his or her eyes on me as the cops and paramedics escorted me to a waiting ambulance. They put me on the gurney, strapped me down, and put me in back. We drove off. The nightmare was just beginning.

Due to a mix-up, they took to the wrong mental hospital. Flat on my back, my arms and legs constrained by the straps, I heard all this confusion. I didn't know what to think or what to feel except fear. Finally we got to the right mental hospital. We went up a service elevator. All the while I was still constrained. All the while I still hadn't spoken.

When we got to the ward, an administrator asked me, "Did you or do you now want to hurt yourself?"

Be calm, I thought to myself. *Be cool*. "No," I answered.

"Did you or do you now want to hurt anyone else?"

"No."

I was put in a room. The nurses didn't know why I was there. All I knew was that I was in a lock-down ward in a psych unit. Five days went by before I was even evaluated by a doctor.

I was there for three months. The setting traumatized me. Many of my wardmates were severely suicidal. The attending psychologists tried to convince me that I was an addict. On television, which we could

----

watch for an hour in the evenings, Nancy Reagan looked into the camera and told us, "Just say no."

Just say what they want you to say, I thought to myself, *and get the hell out of here.*

"I am a substance abuser," I said.

I got out.

Later my mother said she regretted that she and Dave sent me there. I didn't blame them. These were confusing times for everyone. The eighties were rough but fun. It's always fun when you reach the top of the roller coaster . . . and then . . .

MY RELATIONSHIP WITH HEATHER was beautiful but tough. She broke up with me, only to make up and then break up again. This destroyed me. I was certain that our love would be forever, but forever turned out to be little more than a year our first time around—and another year our second time.

When Heather kicked me to the curb two separate times, I swore never to love again. The feeling of exposing my heart and soul—the sensation of utter vulnerability—scared me to death.

Heather's reasons for the breakups made sense. She didn't want to get so serious so soon. She wanted to be free to explore the world without being tied to one guy. Perhaps love wasn't an obsession for her as it was for me. Whatever, I was crushed and vowed to cover my heart with black iron, never to be broken again.

SWING

Brothers and Sisters:

We'd like to thank ya'll for comin' down to see SWING and, as always, we need your support to keep the funk rollin'.

The boys will agree: there's nothin' finer than layin' down the groove for all you folks.

SWING: Scotty (vocals), Corey (guitar), Robert (bass), Britt (keyboards) and Eric (drums); looks forward to seeing you soon!

SWING boys will be droppin' the funk on your bootie:

Wednesday, *June 21st* at **CATCH 22**
Thursday, *July 6th* at the **ROXY**
with **MARY'S DANISH**, 9:00 pm
Saturday, *July 15th*
at **COCANUT TEASZERS**, 9:00 pm

For further info call SWING at (213) 837-2341.
Don't forget to call KROQ at 520-1067 to request Drop the Funk.

NEW KID

in

TOWN

NO MATTER WHAT CLUB WE PLAYED, Soi-Disant brought the party back to one particular frat house that was attached to the University of California at Irvine. We did so for a simple reason: One of the frat members dealt coke.

It was during this period when, at one of our gigs, a tall, skinny bass player came onstage and joined us for a rendition of "Louie Louie," the "Star-Spangled Banner" of rock and roll.

The guy was six foot two, weighed 155 pounds, and was the best bass player I had ever heard. He looked like John Taylor from Duran Duran. His name was Robert DeLeo, and he grew up around the Jersey Shore. He slapped the bass in the mode of the great funksters like Larry Graham of Sly and the Family Stone and Louis Johnson of the Brothers Johnson. In fact, funk was Robert's thing. He was deeply steeped in the various forms of rhythm and blues. He said one of his idols was James Jamerson, the fabulous Motown bassist and founding member of the famous Funk Brothers rhythm section. Jamerson liberated the bass from its previous role as a mere background instrument: He put it out in front, and he showed generations of musicians how the bass, as a creative force, could sculpt the shape of a song as significantly as the guitarist or even the vocalist.

Cory and I didn't know about Jamerson. In fact, we didn't know much about R & B. Robert blew in with the force of a hurricane and brought the wisdom of an old-school teacher. He was rooted in music that was righteous and real. Robert was a madman who could play as well as Flea, the bassist with the Red Hot Chili Peppers. Robert knew Led Zeppelin

ROBERT WAS A MADMAN WHO COULD PLAY AS WELL AS FLEA

inside and out. We loved Robert. And then Robert disappeared. Nothing strange about that. Musicians jump onto the stage and jump off. Some come back, some don't. We would have been thrilled if Robert had returned, but we weren't about to go looking for him. We had our own thing going.

I sailed through high school with a minimum amount of work. I enjoyed history and literature and did well in college-level courses. The advisor said I would easily be admitted to a good four-year college, but I wasn't quite ready for that. I had quit football, wrestling, and all other sports in favor of singing. Soi-Disant was my main passion. I couldn't give it up, but I also couldn't see myself skipping college altogether. My intellectual curiosity was keen. As a compromise, I enrolled in Orange Coast College, a community school.

I dug it. I was a liberal arts major because that let me flow in several different directions—political science, philosophy, great books. I took careful notes during lectures and got caught up in challenging books like *The Closing of the American Mind*. My grade average in high school was C plus; in college it became B plus. With its less restrictive atmosphere, Orange Coast was much more my style than high school. Enrolled in music theory, poetry, and art, I was committed to the liberal arts. Still am.

Ultimately, though, my commitment to music won out over college. It had to. If it didn't, I saw that I wouldn't be able to earn a living making music. I had to give music my all.

That's also the reason Cory and I decided to reimagine our band. If we were going to make it, we needed to get better, which meant getting better players. We decided to move up to Hollywood. Living there, we would have contact with good musicians. Maybe we'd even run into Robert DeLeo.

ART
SCHOOL
GIRL

I got a girlfriend, she goes to art school
I got a art school girlfriend

She left her home from sweet Alabama
Rose, Alabama, for the city, New York City

I got a girlfriend, she goes to parties
Underground parties, Andy Warhol everywhere
She wears the leather, I wear the makeup
We'll never break up, been together for a month

W HEN I MOVED TO HOLLYWOOD in the pre-STP period of my life, I moved with my girlfriend, Mary Ann. She was an art student. But she didn't come from Alabama. I put that in the song, which came out on STP's *Tiny Music* album years later, because it made for a better story. The truth is that Mary Ann was a tough-ass chick from Orange County.

Mary Ann enrolled at Cal Arts while I found a job as a graphic/ paste-up artist for the Los Angeles *Daily Journal*, a legal newspaper. I went through a quick training program and discovered I had the talent to put together a publication in a matter of hours. We moved into an apartment by MacArthur Park near downtown L.A. I didn't know it at the time, but a few years later MacArthur Park would become the place where I'd get lost in the rabbit holes.

I had met Mary Ann at a club just after her boyfriend had moved to Paris. She was crushed, and I was determined to woo her. I loved her looks: strawberry blond hair, pale skin, blue eyes, full lips. She looked Irish but was mainly Lithuanian. I also loved her taste and talent for all things cultural. She was an edgy chick with a fiery personality, a ballet

———————

dancer as well as a student in an arts college in L.A. At the time, I was still living in Huntington Beach, but that didn't stop me from burning up the freeway to spend the night with Mary Ann in her dorm room.

My wooing worked. Mary Ann and I hooked up. While I was trying to make progress in the rock-and-roll game, she was expressing her soul in paintings. Like me, she liked to drink to excess. She has since reformed, but when we lived together in L.A., daily life was wild. Mary Ann was my first type A girlfriend: the first girl to hit me, the first one to torch my car. (Actually, it was my dad's old broken-down car that he had given me.)

After the torching, I asked her why.

"You said I was too much for you," she answered. "You wanted to break up. You broke my heart."

"But is that any reason to burn up a car?"

"Yes, it is," she said. "Be glad I didn't torch you along with the car."

I WAS GLAD.

Glad to return to the challenges of rock and roll.

JANNINA CASTENEDA:

Beautiful woman, beautiful soul, beautiful spirit in my life when my life couldn't appreciate her kind of beauty.

I met Jannina, who had an Ecuadorian mother and Mexican father, when she was nineteen and I was twenty-two. My career was still on stall. I was living off Wilshire Boulevard in mid-city L.A., where I hung out at the King King club at Sixth and La Brea. The Red Devils, a group I dug, often jammed there. Sometimes you might see Jimmie Vaughan performing. It was my kind of hipster scene.

One night I went in for drinks, met a dude named Tony, his sister Jannina, and Jannina's friend Marina. We drank, danced, and brought the party back to our place. At first I was chatting up Marina, but couldn't keep my eyes off Jannina. She was short—five foot three—with a tight, beautiful body; long, deep dark-brown hair; deep-set dark-brown eyes; a Roman nose; a perfect bubble butt; a small overbite that I found alluring; and an aura of sweetness that drew me to her. At the end of the evening, I asked for her number.

"I thought you liked Marina," she said.

"I do, but I have a crush on you."

She gave me her number; a few weeks later she gave me her love. We had much in common: We liked the same kind of music and we were believing Catholics, both from good families, both interested in a long-lasting relationship. Jannina had a good job selling makeup for Clinique at an upscale department store in Pasadena. Earlier in her life she had set her sights on going to the Olympics in gymnastics. A superb athlete, she came close, winning state and national championships. But at a critical point she lost on the balance beam and her dream of Olympic glory was dashed.

HIGH
as the
SUN

T HE BIGGEST MUSICAL CHALLENGE I had was facing the truth: I had to upgrade the quality of the musicians I was playing with. Cory agreed. But deep down, I also knew that Cory, for all his talent, wasn't really up to the task of the major-league music biz. At the same time, he agreed that we needed to recruit Robert DeLeo.

Robert was still on the musical scene, so it wasn't hard to find him. When I did, I put it to him plainly: "Join our band."

Robert was reluctant. "I don't want to play with Britt."

"I understand," I said. "We'll get a new guy on keyboards."

"I don't think we need keyboards," said Robert. "And I know he's your close buddy, but I also don't think we need Cory."

"You will tell Britt he's out?"

"Yes," Robert agreed, "if you tell Cory."

Thus the seeds of STP were sown.

Cory was cool about it. He sensed it was coming. He had tears in his eyes, but realized our ambition was greater than his. Britt wasn't as cool. He felt duped.

———————

NO MATTER, ROBERT AND I WERE MOVING AHEAD. Eric Kretz, a superb musician, became our drummer. All we lacked was a killer lead guitarist. Robert had only briefly mentioned his brother Dean. He never promoted him. All he said was, "The best fuckin' guitarist I know is my big brother."

The trouble was that Dean, who had moved from Jersey to San Diego, was no longer playing. He was a super-successful businessman who had married his high school girlfriend and bought a beautiful home. When Robert and I joined forces, Dean helped us get gigs down in San Diego—that's one of the reasons we got a reputation as a San Diego band—but he didn't play with us. We'd all party at his house afterward. He was generous with his encouragement, but it took a long time to convince him to break out his guitar and jam.

Once he did, though, our lives were never the same. Our first jam with Dean was on a riff that became "Where the River Goes" on *Core.*

I wanna be big as a mountain
I wanna fly high as the sun
I wanna know what the rent's like in heaven
I wanna know where the river goes

To us, Dean's playing was big as a mountain and high as the sun. He pushed us up to a heavenly plane. Whatever had happened to him in the past—however he had become disillusioned or disheartened—the power of the music we made together pushed him out of retirement.

For months he was just our friend in San Diego, our bassist's brother, a superhip guy who helped us book gigs. And then, with one jam, he became an integral part of the band. This was the late eighties, but Dean was essential seventies, a guitar worthy of Zeppelin. Musically, physically, spiritually, he was perfect for the part. Genetically engineered to be a guitar player, he was a gangly guy with thick, unruly hair, an oversize mouth, oversize lips, thundering chops. He was a skinny motherfucker, but he could play!

THUNDERING CHOPS

Beyond what might seem like a stereotype, he was a real person whose charisma drew everyone—including me—to his side. Jack Kerouac had his Dean Moriarty. I had my Dean DeLeo. His mantra was, "Everything in moderation, even moderation." Like Keith Richards, he was a glorious rogue.

The DeLeos' dad died young, and Dean became father to Robert: Even during his crazy high school days, Dean maintained a sense of responsibility. If I brought him the dark news of punk culture, he brought me the complete grammar of gunslingin' guitarists, from Muddy Waters and Wes Montgomery to Jimi Hendrix and Jimmy Page.

Mighty Joe Young, May 7, 1990, at Club Lingerie, Hollywood, CA. From left to right: Robert DeLeo, Scott, Eric Kretz (drums), Corey Hickock (Photo by Bobby Devine)

SUMMER

of

MARY

J ANNINA CASTENEDA WAS THERE FIRST. I fell for her, and then I fell for Mary Forsberg. Mary went away. Jannina stayed. Mary came back, only to go away again and then return. All the while, filled with guilt and passion, I tormented myself, making one ill-fated decision after another.

NOW I REINTRODUCE MARY FORSBERG—blessed Mary, mother of two beautiful children, the love of my early dreams, the woman who overwhelmed my heart and my head for much of my life.

It was the dawn of the nineties. I had just turned twenty-three. Eric Kretz, Dean and Robert DeLeo, and I had an unsigned band called Mighty Joe Young. I needed work and took a job as a driver for a modeling agency. Robert worked at a music store, right across the street from the agency. He'd come over with ideas for songs—chords, melodies, riffs. Words and stories started coming to me as well. "Plush." "Creed." "Wicked Garden." We were doing live shows and had developed a strong following in San Diego as well as Hollywood. On any given night, we could draw two hundred people. For an unsigned band, that was good. We got gigs opening for Rollins Band, Ice T, and Soul Asylum.

———————

I was a young man driving beautiful young models to their jobs in my old '65 Chrysler Imperial Crown. My job paid eight dollars an hour, not so bad for those times. Before that, I was mainly being supported by my beautiful girlfriend Jannina. I never thought that driving models would lead to high drama. If you had asked me, I would have naïvely said, "It's good work. They let me off when I have a gig or have to rehearse. I like these people. The girls are beautiful. They're all my age or younger. But models being interested in me? No way. They have a lot more going on than me."

It was a good summer. I was living with Dean in Highland Park, a funky part of L.A. It was a summer of barbecues and beer, a summer in a kicked-back Mexican neighborhood, a summer of possibilities. That same summer we learned that Mighty Joe Young was the name of a blues singer who was still working. His management asked us to drop the handle. Blues ethos required that we respect our fellow musician, so we began searching for another name.

It was also the summer of my shrine, a makeshift holy spot lit by candles and surrounded by tchotchkes. It was a summer of waiting for the muse to bless us with songs. In the center of the shrine I placed a can of STP oil treatment. It was there for comfort. As a kid, I had STP stickers on my bike. I loved the brand. I loved the way Richard Petty, a fantastic character, was rock-and-roll hell on wheels. He wore the STP logo. Those letters represented it all—rebelliousness, chance victory, going for broke. I saw it as serendipitous. I loved the clarity and directness of the label. Maybe it could work for us. If it was good enough for Richard Petty—who, after all, was the Keith Richards of car racing—then hell, it was good enough for us.

But what would it stand for?

Shirley Temple's Pussy. The name was thrown around just for humor's sake. We worried, though, that the all-American macho males who were consuming this new brand of alt rock might not get the sarcasm. So the long process of searching for a name continued.

The shrine I built to keep evil out.
I think it brought the evil in.

Meanwhile, models had to be driven. One day I was told to drive a girl called Mary. She was sixteen. She lived with a Vietnamese gay man, an agent with her agency. Mary was stunning, a San Diego surfer girl aglow with the light of a cloudless sky. Long flowing natural golden brown hair with streaks bleached by the California sun. Her beauty was otherworldly, almost painful. She carried a pain I couldn't name. She was painfully shy, said hardly a word. Our pain collided, but silently. Pain wasn't expressed, only sensed.

Mary and I worked for Nicole Bordeaux, owner of the modeling agency, a woman who reminded me of Cruella De Vil from 101 *Dalmatians*, except she wasn't cruel. She was fabulous and flamboyant and protective of her girls. Her husband, David Bordeaux, had taken *her* name, a fact I found amusing. The modeling business moved on frenetic energy, the kind fueled by coke. It was all about free champagne and go-for-broke nightclubs. Nicole regarded me as just another would-be rocker in some unknown band. You could find thousands of us on every block of Hollywood or in the pages of LA *Weekly*. Yet Nicole was careful to select me as Mary's driver.

"She isn't one of my skyscraper models," she said, referring to Mary. "She's a young, delicate creature. She doesn't have a driver's license yet. Handle her with care. She's our Kate Moss."

When Mary walked in wearing a backpack, her appearance belied her beauty. She wore no makeup, simple jeans, a white T-shirt. Her lips were large and sensuous, her sculpted cheekbones high, her eyes a deep, rich brown. She was no taller than five foot eight. When Nicole introduced her to me, I thought I caught the shadow of a smile. I couldn't be sure.

As she walked toward me, she didn't say anything. As I drove her to her gig, the silence held steady. I wondered if she was shy or simply had

little to say. I tried some easy conversation. She answered monosyllabi-
cally. I stopped trying.

"Wanna listen to the Beastie Boys or Nirvana?" I asked.

"Sure," she said.

Paul's Boutique sounded good, even on my shitty car stereo.

When I picked up Mary after her modeling session, she seemed glad
to see me but didn't say so. I slipped in a cassette of Nirvana's *Nevermind*.
This was 1991, and the record had started a tidal wave of things to come.
The wave was glorious, but the tide brought destruction.

"Please make that louder," she said.

I gladly complied. Mary was feeling
what I was feeling—at least I thought so. We
started getting closer. She was just getting
out of a relationship, and I was in one with
Jannina. I loved Jannina, but, having met
Mary, realized that I was never *in* love with
Jannina. What's the difference? I could answer
with a single word—obsession. I see love, like
art, as an obsession. Maybe that's an overly
romantic view of human existence, but I'm
an overly romantic human being. If love, like
rock and roll, doesn't consume me 24-7, it's
not love. It can be respect, appreciation, ad-
miration, wonderment, it can be a world of
glory and a lifetime of peace, but I can't call
it love. Love burns me and confuses me.
Love's a light that can't be extinguished.

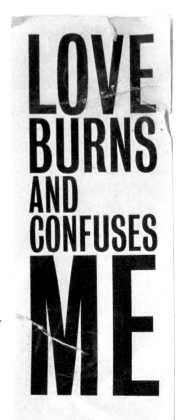

Mary had this light in her eyes; her eyes were filled with love. She also had darkness. She kept a book of her modeling photographs that I took home and studied. I placed it in a drawer. Jannina found the book and asked me about it. I fumbled and fidgeted. "It was in the car," I said. "I brought it inside by mistake." My lie was apparent. I was raised not to lie, so I'm not good at it. But love's obsession broke down my moral code. Love's obsession had me dreaming of Mary.

When I came to pick her up one morning, the front door to her apartment was open. "Come in," she said. Fresh from a shower, she had a towel wrapped around her body. I sat on the bed, embarrassed. I wanted to kiss her, but didn't.

Mary's moods. Mary's expressions. Mary saying to me, "Would you mind if I asked you to put on my makeup? I'm not too good at that."

The long, hot summer passed and we still didn't kiss. It was all looks and gestures, nothing but sensuous silence.

Putting on her makeup was the most sensuous moment I had ever experienced with her yet. Tenderly moving ruby red lipstick across her lips. Powdering her cheeks. Slowly applying eyeliner.

Wanting to kiss her.

Wanting to hold her.

Wanting to say something—and instead saying nothing.

Later I learned that Mary also wanted to say something. Later she said that she too wanted to kiss me and hold me. She said she was waiting for me to make my move. But no move was made that summer.

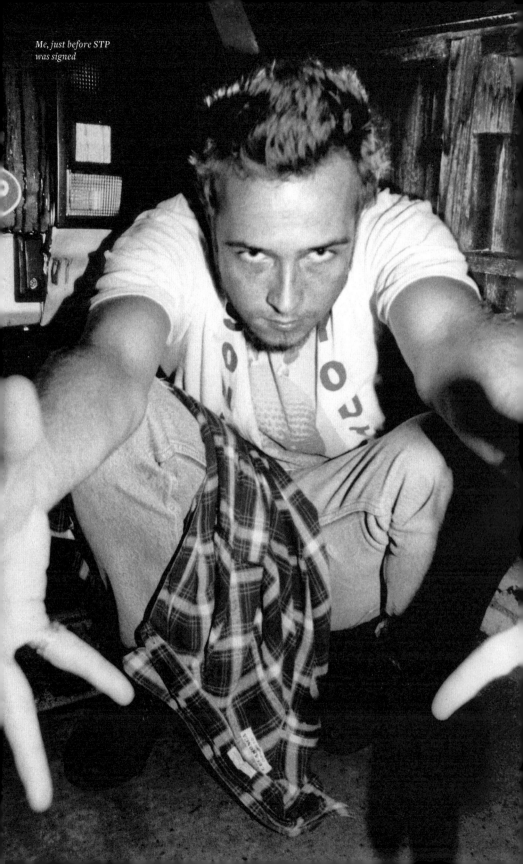

Me, just before STP was signed

SUMMER

of

MUSIC

W E FELL IN LOVE WITH THE STP LOGO and just needed a name to go with it. Stone Temple Pilots seemed to fit the bill. It sounded adventuresome; it sounded strange; it sounded like us. It was a blazing summer of beer and pot parties. Our band was beginning to catch the wave of alternative energy sweeping over the music business. Within a few months, STP, Tool, and Rage Against the Machine all got deals with major labels. Our deal came as a result of three shows. The first had us opening for Body Count, Ice T's band, at the Palladium. The second saw us opening for the Rollins Band at the Whiskey. That was the gig where we had a few girls dress up in semi-bondage gear and blow bubbles. Mary was one of those girls. Our relationship, though, remained chaste.

The third gig was the most important—the Shamrock, a dive in Silver Lake. It was there the offer was made. Tom Carolan, an A&R exec at Atlantic, said, "You guys are great! How would you like to make a record for us?" We acted as though we had managers and advisors to contact. But of course we were going to make a record for Atlantic. We were shocked into a state of manic bliss. Atlantic was the ideal label. Founded by Ahmet Ertegun, it had started out as an indie and wound up signing Ray Charles, Aretha Franklin, and Led Zeppelin, not to mention the Rolling Stones.

We pinched ourselves, realizing it was a combination of blind ambition and musical talent that put us on the treadmill to big-time success. We were ecstatic, but we were also dead serious about crafting

CRITICAL FLOP

and playing the kind of self-reflective rock that we respected. We weren't going to do crap; and we weren't going to be imitators. We thought we had an original voice, original stories, and an original sound. We wanted to get to the essential elements of what we were all about— the core of our music—so we called the record *Core*. We had merged our musical sensibilities and forged something new. Of course we had influences—the Stones, Pink Floyd, Metallica, the Beatles, Zep, and a dozen other bands. But the whole of STP turned out to be far greater than the sum of our parts; it turned out to be visceral—a little strange, sometimes lyrical, and always intense. We loved *Core*.

The critics hated it; the critics pulverized us; the critics loved pulverizing us. Today, I can talk about the critics' murderous response to our work with a certain distance. Today, I don't give a shit. But back then, I cared. I was a serious musician looking for serious critics to take us seriously. Robert, Eric, and especially Dean, who was superserious about rock history, felt the same. So when the writers dumped on us, it was a definite drag. I actually called Danny Goldberg, the president of Atlantic, to explain my plight and point. He said, "Don't worry. I used to be the publicist for Zeppelin, and, for their first years, it was the same for them. Now look at how they're viewed—as legends."

Critical flop but commercial smash—that's the story of *Core*. The record started selling, and, some eight million copies later, has never stopped. Neither did the critics stop criticizing. "Sex Type Thing," a big hit single off the record, was characterized by some closed-minded morons as a date-rape song. Some actually said that we were *promoting* date rape. Because the song was written in the voice of the deranged character, there were critics who presumed I was that character. That's like saying that there's no difference between a first-person character created by a writer and the writer himself. The assumption is ridiculous. I wanted to point out the craziness of that criticism, so before getting out onstage and performing "Sex Type Thing," I smeared lipstick across my mouth and slipped on a dress.

It was a big moment. After MTV's *Spring Break*, we flew across the pond for a couple of days of promotion and concerts. The drag version of "Sex Type Thing" became performance art. After a few bars of the song clicked in, we saw the openmouthed, wide-eyed looks from all the shirtless macho men in the crowd. But then, even though I'm not sure those guys got our irony, they started slam dancing, moshing, and crowd surfing—a big hint that we were beginning to make waves. We felt justified. Our message was getting across...AMEN!

COMMERCIAL SMASH

Halloween night. As you can see, I'm the one who looks like Cheryl Tiegs.

"I SEE
that
THESE
are
LIES
to
COME"

—*from "Plush"*

1992. WE WERE TOURING AND "SEX TYPE THING"

was out as a single. The tour consisted of us taking turns driving an RV while crisscrossing the country playing small clubs. Our first show was in Orange County with my Huntington Beach friends cheering me on. On my twenty-fourth birthday, we were in the middle of nowhere, so we camped out for the night. Robert made us tuna burgers, we got crazy drunk, and had a ball. The world was still young and fresh. We were still indestructible.

Sometimes at our concerts we got concerned at the number of skinheads in the crowd. I hated that. They weren't who we wanted to perform for. Whatever energy we were exerting was not meant to stimulate them. "If you don't want this vibe," I'd say, "go to a Pantera concert."

In New York, where we didn't have much of a following, we played at a place called the Bank at Houston and Ludlow. A few years later I'd be scoring dope at that very corner. But for now, we were just trying to score with the music industry. Metal radio was playing us—"Sex Type Thing" was seen as a metal song—and that both bugged and pleased us. It bugged us

because we didn't see ourselves as metal. It pleased us because we were on the radio. And besides, the same thing was happening to Soundgarden and Nirvana. If they could be confused for heavy metal, why not STP?

Down in New Orleans, we found ourselves in the wrong neighborhood in the wrong hotel but were too dumb to know. We kept partying.

One night Dean drank too much and got sick all over the RV. Robert came waltzing into the hotel room with the new Stray Cats record and said, "Now I know why they called it *Choo Choo Hot Fish*." Dean spent hours cleaning up his puke.

Little by little, the record started catching fire until we got word that MTV's *Headbangers Ball* wanted to interview us. That's when Dean and I bonded big-time. Rather than be interviewed, Dean suggested that he bring his acoustic guitar to the MTV studios in New York so we could perform an acoustic version of "Plush."

We were overstimulated from touring and, to sleep on the plane, we took a handful of powerful pills—my first—that coated our brains and numbed out the world. When we got to the fancy hotel in New York, I vomited in the lobby. Dean barely made it up to the room before he vomited all over the bathroom. When we got to MTV at six that morning, we were high as zombies, and yet . . .

Dean played his most heartbreakingly soulful version of "Plush"—and I sang it with more relaxed feeling than ever before or since. It was chill and it was mellow, an acoustic statement still being played on radio stations some eighteen years later. This is a story that seems to have a somewhat happy ending. It is a false ending, however, because my story only became more painful.

WHEN CORE FINALLY BEGAN TO FLY, it soared, generating four top-five hits, two of which went to number one. I remember management or the label or someone in a suit coming to us and saying, "It's happened! The big break is here! Aerosmith wants you to open for them!"

I looked at Dean, Robert, and Eric, and saw the same expression on their face that was on mine.

"No," we said. "That's the worst thing that could happen to us. We're not opening for Aerosmith."

WINTER
of our
DISCONTENT

F REEZING-COLD LONDON IN THE WINTER OF '93.
Core had blown up beyond anyone's wildest dreams. We were nonstop traveling, promoting, selling records.

This was our first tour outside the United States. It had been many months since I'd seen Mary. She was now seventeen and emancipated from her parents after having left them in California. I hadn't forgotten her, but I had disciplined myself not to call. Suddenly my discipline collapsed. I called L.A. I learned she had switched agencies and was working in Paris but, miracle of miracles, she happened to be in London at this very moment. My mind went crazy. This couldn't be coincidence. This was fate. Fuck cupids! We were brought together by Aphrodite herself.

I called her and asked, "Would you come to my hotel?"

"Yes."

Mary arrived wrapped in wool. She glowed. She kissed me on the cheek. The hotel had a private bar, small and intimate. Our chitchat was small and intimate. She explained how she had sued for her independence from her parents and was completely on her own. Mary looked sensational. In the year since I had seen her, she had traveled the world.

———————

She had done shows in New York, Tokyo, and London. She was confident, she radiated sophisticated energy, she was irresistible.

"You're a whole new person," I said.

"You are too. You've become a star."

Her words were still few, but they were all the right words.

She asked me if I wanted her to walk me to my room.

"You can stay over if you like," I said. "I'll sleep on the couch."

She stayed, and I didn't sleep on the couch. Our sexual connection was even more powerful than I had anticipated. We became one. The heavens opened.

"Go on this tour with me," I said. "Stay."

For five days she stayed with me as the bus bounced through the hills and hedgerows of England and Germany. At the end of the fifth day, she had to go back to work.

"I am in love with you," she said.

I was in love with her, and I told her so.

"What will happen now?" she asked.

"I don't know."

SUMMER
KISS

I DIDN'T GET HIGH—not seriously high—till the next summer. We were back in the States, still promoting *Core*, this time on tour with Butthole Surfers, Flaming Lips, Firehose, and Basehead. This was the Barbecue Mitzvah Tour. By then we were the hot band—the majority of the fans were coming to see *us*—but out of respect for the alternative founding fathers Butthole Surfers and Flaming Lips, whose current hit was "She Don't Use Jelly," we only co-headlined.

The tour was drug-heavy and sex-heavy. I couldn't see myself passing up the delicacies that came with being a rock star—cocaine, alcohol, Lady Lay. So we rolled into New York, where we stayed at the Royalton Hotel. There was something deadly decadent about the place. What the Hollywood Hyatt House—the one called the Riot House—had been to an earlier rock generation, the Royalton was to ours. It was decidedly postmodern, low-key, high-energy sleek, a place where heroin-thin models melted into the dark walls and mirrors. Everything about the hotel made you—made me, made all of us—want to get high.

Mary was in New York. She had been befriended by the magician David Blaine. She had turned eighteen. We hadn't seen each other for a while. That afternoon she came to the hotel. Her mere presence excited me, renewed all my feelings, had me wanting to be with her and her alone. We went shopping for vintage clothes. I spotted a scarlet dress at a boutique in SoHo. When she tried it on, we drifted into a noir from 1947.

"I'll wear it tonight," she said.

"Perfect."

Back at the hotel, I told her good-bye, arranged for her tickets to the concert, promised that we'd meet afterward, and took a nap.

That same day, a few of the musicians had put in their orders for bags of China White. I had never shot or snorted heroin before. But I had studied heroin culture. The truth is that I loved heroin culture. I was intrigued by it.

I had a friend in high school who was a junkie. I loved the work of William S. Burroughs and the brilliance of Charlie Parker. I loved the aesthetic of the Rolling Stones. I knew about John Lennon's heroin period. In the mid-eighties, I had been greatly influenced by Perry Farrell and Jane's Addiction.

FREE-FLOATING MAN IN SPACE

I associated heroin with romance, glamour, danger, and rock-and-roll excess. More than that, I was curious about the connection between heroin and creativity. At that point, I couldn't imagine my life, especially now that I was entering into the major leagues of alternative rock, without at least dabbling with the King of Drugs. So I put in my order.

That night, just for the hell of it, STP dressed up as Kiss. We had the one-piece suits, the black wigs, and the makeup applied by a former Kiss employee. Before hitting the stage, I snorted the China White. The opiate took me to where I'd always dreamed of going. I can't name the place, but I can say that I was undisturbed and unafraid, a free-floating man in a space without demons and doubts. The show was beautiful. The high was beautiful.

The thing about heroin, at least for me, was that I used to be afraid or ultra-self-conscious when I walked into a bar or club. But on dope I could be Superman or any man. I didn't care what anyone thought of me. Dope was my savior. The ultimate equalizer, or so I thought.

After the show, I didn't want to talk to or see a single solitary soul. It's not that I didn't want to see Mary in her scarlet dress or didn't want to revisit our noir movie. I simply had to be alone with this feeling.

"What should I tell Mary?" my roadie asked. "She's waiting for you."

"Tell her I have food poisoning."

It was a shitty excuse, and Mary knew it was a lie. Mary always knew my lies. There was this karmic thing between us. We were drawn to each other like shipwreck survivors. I had never heard a woman speak so openly of depression, for example. When Mary spoke that way, I was riveted by the sadness; I was riveted by her extreme moods, riveted by her needs, her fears, her beauty, her hunger for me, my hunger for her.

Mary herself, by the way, never admitted to a lie. She had a motto for it: "If you get caught, lie lie lie!"

IT WAS AT MY FRIEND RICH CONKLIN'S APARTMENT that a sympathetic woman heard me complain I was coming down with some sickness I couldn't name. A veteran of the "wars," she simply said, "Oh, honey, you're dope sick." So I left the party in a hurry and drove downtown. That's where I scored a package with an intriguing design: a smiling baby riding a dragon through the clouds while a group of angelic ladies looked on with wonder. The package contained China White. The design became the cover of *Purple*, the second STP record.

This was the first and last time I ever found white dope in L.A. The heroin was always black tar from Mexico.

PURPLE
WOUNDS

———

THEY EASE
the PAIN

I N LOVE WITH MARY FROM A DISTANCE, living with Jannina up close. Guilt was my best friend, my worst enemy, my motivator, and my tormentor.

Free from time, suspended in space.

Purple was recorded outside of time and space, inside Atlanta, where I found a drug dealer down in funky town. She was twenty-five and, unfortunately, HIV positive. Her boyfriend was a death rocker with a death wish. Kurt Cobain was still alive. Grunge, as they labeled it, was still king—of music, social awareness, and even high fashion.

I was living to score because my habit had me sick and the downers and barbiturates weren't getting me well. The girl with AIDS was my key to heroin health. I got my bags of good shit and my clean rigs; I was cool to record. We cut and mixed the whole album in less than a month. Then it was back to L.A., where my fucking habit, begun on the Barbecue Mitzvah Tour, had grown up into a big black monster.

Jannina and I had moved into a house in remote and rustic Topanga Canyon, a world away from the nasty streets that sold the stuff I craved. I had to stop. I planned to wean off. By the second day, though, I failed and was flying high. I knew I needed bodily health, knew I needed to detox. I found a rehab place in Marina del Rey called Exodus. Just as I was about to check in, I was told not to. Kurt Cobain and Gibby Haynes were there.

Gibby was my Butthole Surfer buddy from the Barbecue Mitzvah Tour, where we had gone off the rails. My business manager didn't think it was a good idea for us to be together, so I went to a treatment center in Pasadena where, two days later, I learned that Kurt had left Exodus. Four days after that I was told that Kurt was dead. The news frightened and devastated me, driving me into more dark solitude. The news had me searching all the silent places in my brain for explanations and comfort. This was April of 1994.

Confusing matters more was the sensational success of *Purple*. After trashing *Core*, the critics finally came our way and embraced *Purple*, validating STP as a legitimate rock band with an artistic attitude all our own. The public also dug it. When the record dropped in June of that same year, it debuted at number one. "Interstate Love Song" was a huge hit. So were "Vasoline" and "Big Empty," which said, "Too much walkin', shoes worn thin . . . too much trippin', and my soul's worn thin."

We went on tour. Europe was cool, but Germany was freezing cold. We were set to fly back to the States and do MTV's *Spring Break* in Florida. Hungry for sunshine, we planned on arriving a few days before the show. But our manager pushed back our departure date due to our obligation to do major press in Germany. But we eventually made it to Florida.

The big thrill there was a woman I'll call Alison. She was an edgy photographer. Dean and I were both drawn to her. She was blond, sexy, a little older, and a hard-core junkie. No, there was no three-way. I did, however, form a bond with Alison that lasted quite awhile.

Alison was an intriguingly talented hot mess. She could hang with the boys and talk trash. She was big fun for the funksters, with no strings attached. Alison had a longer relationship with dope than I did. We barely crossed narcotic paths; our get-high times together were few. She was a far more advanced student of the scene. I learned from her in many ways. She lived at the fertile crossroads of art and dope. Miraculously, though, Alison got clean while I stayed stuck in the mud and murk for years to come.

Now it was 1995, the year that should have been the best year of my life. It was the worst. I was busted for possession. I faced a trial for drug possession, where I got three years suspended sentence and five months in drug jail. And STP fell apart.

Headlining at Madison Square Garden — Aerosmith joined us onstage

"WHAT'S REAL?
WHAT'S *for* SALE?"

—from "Vasoline"

I LIKE PURPLE MORE THAN CORE. For all it strengths, *Core* was a little bit of a production compromise. Because we knew what we were doing in terms of song stylings and studio sounds, *Purple* was more honest and more autobiographical. It was also more heartfelt and heartsick.

"Vasoline," for example, is about being stuck in the same situation over and over again. It's about me becoming a junkie. It's about lying to Jannina and lying to the band about my heroin addiction. "You search for things," I wrote, "that you can't see. Going blind, out of reach, somewhere in the Vasoline."

"Unglued" hits the same theme. I'm hooked. "I got this thing," I sing, "it's coming over me. Moderation is masturbation . . . this confusion is my illusion . . . all these things I'm sick about . . . I kick about . . . always come unglued."

"Pretty Penny" is still another drug story, a mother-daughter junkie team who are "blown away and lost the pearl and price [they] paid."

"Interstate Love Song" was written about the phone calls I had with Jannina. She'd ask how I was doing, and I'd lie, say I was doing fine. Chances are I had just fixed before calling her. I imagined what was going through her mind when I wrote, "Waiting on a Sunday afternoon for what I read

---

between the lines, your lies, feelin' like a hand in rusted shame, so do you laugh or does it cry? Reply?"

And yet I sincerely missed her, sincerely felt for her. Those romantic feelings were expressed in a song for Jannina I called "Still Remains": "Pick a song and sing a yellow nectarine . . . take a bath, I'll drink the water that you leave . . . if you should die before me, ask if you can bring a friend, pick a flower, hold your breath, and drift away."

The record also reflected my feelings about the mish-mash state of the music business. Everyone seemed to be living or dying but making real money.

When the record was finished, a music writer asked me, "Why did you call it *Purple?*"

"Because it sounds purple," I said. "Besides, that's a stupid question. Why is your rag called *Spin?*"

AFTER *PURPLE* WAS FINALLY FINISHED, I came home to Topanga Canyon emotionally distraught and incredibly needy. I needed something steady; I needed to be cared for. I took Jannina down to the beach and asked her to marry me.

She said yes and suggested that the wedding take place in her aunt and uncle's beautiful home in San Marino, the exclusive old-money section of Pasadena where the streets are lined with mansions. The wedding was extravagant—family, friends, music moguls. I snuck off with the grooms-men to do coke in the limo. My friend Eddie Nichols, the singer for Royal Crown Revue, sang "Stormy Weather," a good indication of what lay ahead.

Jannina and I went to the Greek isles for our honeymoon and stayed in an ancient white alcove in the side of a mountain. After a few days of drinking homemade ouzo, we flew off to Cancún and swam in the warm water. I was still in the process of kicking heroin and had enough morphine sulfate pills and Vicodin to get me through.

Back home, Jannina got really sick and wound up in the hospital, where they gave her a shot of morphine. At the time I was two months clean, but viewing her injection set off sirens in my head, especially when I saw such peace and calm come over her face. I left the hospital to look for my dealer. An hour later, I was loaded.

Nonetheless, we pursued the dream of domestic happiness. From her aunt and uncle, we bought the home in which we were married—Jannina's dream home—and began to live a life of luxury, collecting antiques and cars.

DREAM OF DOMESTIC HAPPINESS

A YEAR LATER, I GOT HOME FROM TOURING behind *Purple* and was promptly arrested close to my home in Pasadena for trying to score. I was getting sloppy.

Jannina bailed me out. "I'm dope sick," I told her. "You gotta get me well. You gotta get me to my dealer. Then we'll make a plan for me to kick, but first I've gotta get well."

"No," said Jannina. "Fuck that. I will not take you to your dealer. I hate that bitch!"

I got into our '65 Mustang convertible with Jannina behind the wheel. I begged her to change her mind.

"It's my medicine," I said to her. "I need my medicine."

Jannina wouldn't budge. I was desperate. As the car made a right turn going 10 or 15 miles an hour, I jumped out, hit the ground, and started rolling. Jannina didn't look back. Jannina had had enough. I was so sick I'd do anything to score—fuckin' anything. I found a payphone and called my one hope, the lady who'd been supplying me. In my mind, I knew I had a fifty-fifty chance of finding her at home.

She picked up the phone! Fuck, I was relieved!

"You gotta come here and get me," I pleaded. "You gotta pick me up."

"No way. If you want it, come get it."

I came in a cab. The fare, plus the cost of the dope, exhausted my funds. All I had left was an ATM card. Loaded, I made it over to the Chateau Marmont, the old-school Hollywood hotel where artists came to live or die. That's where I ran into another one of my dealer's best customers, Courtney Love. She was with Amanda de Cadenet, the photographer/ socialite. As fate would have it, their room was next to mine. That night Courtney and I got high as she and Amanda dressed for dinner at the home of Jack Nicholson. For a while, Ms. Love inserted herself into my ever-more-erratic story. We were never lovers but were rather close at the start. She was this intriguing character who required constant attention.

When, for example, she nodded out on dope, she never failed to do so sitting in a chair and spreading her legs wide. I kept hearing the Stones singing, "Oh yeah, she's a starfucker, starfucker, starfucker, starfucker!"

When word of my arrest in Pasadena became public, I was still living at the Marmont and partying hard. The press was asking me for a statement concerning my drug bust. I didn't want to go on TV, so I wrote something and gave it to Courtney to read on my behalf. She was delighted to be my spokesperson. In essence, I said that I would never advocate drugs for anyone, that I was not in great shape but hoping to get better.

It was not a particularly strong statement, but at that point I was not a particularly strong man. I was groping, grieving, and getting more fucked up on heroin, a drug that simultaneously made me feel bad, feel good, and feel bad for feeling good. Confusion reigned. The din inside my brain was louder than the din of a dozen metal bands. Only heroin could turn up the quiet. Only heroin took me to the place where shame, guilt, and remorse were magically washed away.

"BREATHING
is the
HARDEST
THING"

*—from "Interstate
Love Song"*

I N 1995, STILL HEAVILY HOOKED, I started recording the third STP record, *Tiny Music . . . Songs from the Vatican Gift Shop*. That happened in famed film actor Jimmy Stewart's enormous mansion in Santa Barbara. We had everything we wanted—total privacy, private cook, absolute tranquility. Given the most sumptuous surroundings to make music, though, rockers can turn heaven into hell. At least I can. Artistically, Dean, Robert, Eric, and I were on the same page. We wanted to make a statement. We wanted to deconstruct, go low-tech, get to the dark heart of the matter. I was happy to write Bowie-esque stream-of-consciousness lyrics that didn't need to make sense. Example: "Big Bang Baby":

> *Does anybody know how the story really goes*
> *Or should we all just hum along*
> *Sell your soul and sign an autograph*
> *Big bang baby, crash crash crash*
> *I wanna die but I gotta laugh*
> *Orange crush mama is a laugh laugh laugh*

The laugh, though, was on me. I was at the height—or depth—of my addiction. Shooting coke. Shooting heroin. Running down the 101 every third day to L.A. to score and running back. Jannina called me all the time. Where was I? What was I doing? I was worrying her to death. "Don't worry," I said. "I'm fine."

When STP decided to fly out to Atlanta to finish up the record, I brought along Jannina's brother Tony, who, although high, was not insanely high like me—just insanely more of a drunk. I was getting increasingly paranoid. When Tony needed a break, I brought out my pal Ron Kaufman to see after me. But no one could really help. When I passed out in front of the hotel in the limo, no one could wake me up. I was passed out in the backseat for six straight hours.

In many respects, *Tiny Music* is a dark record.

"Lady Picture Show," one of the central songs, is about the horrific gang rape of a dancer who winds up falling in love but can't let go of the pain.

"Trippin' on a Hole in a Paper Heart" reflects my hunger for redemption. "Break your neck with diamond noose," I wrote. "It's the last you'll ever choose. I am I am, I said I'm not myself, but I'm not dead and not for sale. Hold me closer, closer, let me go, let me be, just let me be."

"Adhesive" is me at my most depressive moment. "Adhesive" is the bottom: "Comatose commodity. The superhero's dying. All the children crying. Sell more records if I'm dead. Purple flowers once again. Hope it's sooner, hope it's near. Corporate records, fiscal year . . . Stitch the womb and wet the bed. With a whisper I'll be dead."

WHEN *TINY MUSIC* CAME OUT, some critics said it was influenced by the rock band Redd Kross. The critics weren't entirely wrong. After *Purple*, we had toured with Redd Kross. When I was in my late teens and early twenties, I was certainly a Redd Kross fan.

Eddie Kurdziel, superb Redd Kross guitarist and friend of Dean's and mine, became a casualty of the nineties. He died of an overdose in 1999. Did our fascination with heroin influence Eddie's decision to try it? I can't say for sure. I suspect, though, that it did. And if that's the case, I am deeply sorry.

Redd Kross had a whimsical, sometimes frivolous attitude that I admired. They were Beatles-influenced, just as we were. I had been lovingly and carefully studying the Beatles for years. You could say the same thing about Cheap Trick, who opened for us during a segment of the *Tiny Music* tour. Our influences came from everywhere. If your hearts and ears are open—as ours were—you absorb the world around you.

Core had happened
Purple had happened.
Tiny Music had happened.
Heroin had happened.
Jannina had happened.
Mary had happened.
Money had happened.
Fame had happened.

The more I got, the more I lost. The more I lost, the more I wanted. The more I wanted, the more I wasted. The more I wasted, the more I wandered. And wondered. I took to the streets, the alleyways, the dark passages that connected me to death and death's closest friends.

"CONFUSION
IS MY
ILLUSION"

—*from "Unglued"*

S TP—A MUSICAL PHENOMENON. A cultural breakthrough. *Rolling Stone* cover. Thirteen rehab stints in three years. This is the 1996–1997 run behind *Tiny Music*.

The guys—Robert, Dean, Eric—knew I was hurting. "We're your brothers," they said. "Just tell us what's happening. We don't want to hear about it in the papers. We want you to come to us first."

Brotherhood. Solidarity. Money on the line. We had a million dollars lined up for a gig in Anchorage and two in Hawaii. After we played Jay Leno's *Tonight Show*, I gathered up my courage and talked to Dean, Robert, and Eric, man to man.

"Okay, guys," I said. "I'll level with you. I've been chipping. But I have enough meds to get me through these gigs. And I'll bring a sober guy along with me, at my expense, to make sure I stay straight."

Next thing I know, my own Stoned Brother Pilots call a press conference and cancel the gigs, telling the world, in essence, that because of their junkie lead singer, the tour can't go on.

It was a vicious move, even more so when "our" lawyers demanded that I pay *them*—out of *my* own pocket—the million dollars caused by the cancellation.

I was through. I was out.

I was back in rehab.

I was out of rehab.

I was back on dope.

I was married to Jannina and, in one of these half-recovered states, went home to find her with another man. She cried, she apologized, she felt terrible, but I felt worse. I said, "Look, the way I've treated you, this is hardly your fault."

The marriage was over. The divorce took forever and cost me a fortune.

"I'M a SELFISH PIECE of SHIT"

—*from "Barbarella"*

F AR AS BANDS GO, I'VE ALWAYS BEEN HALF OUT AND HALF IN. My nature is that of an individual artist. I can get excited about joining the team and going for the gold; I can even be a gung ho team player, but not for long. No doubt, STP was born out of my soul—and the souls of Robert, Dean, and Eric. As I write, STP is completing a new record, and the reunion feels good, even organic, because the band's initial impulse had genuine artistic merit. I expect that STP, as both a recording and touring band, will endure. Our relationship to our fans is based on a shared passion and a history that is nearly twenty years old. Creatively, we continue to inspire one another and my hope is that we all grow old together, but just not in tight leather pants. I prefer a more graceful approach—Bryan Ferry, David Bowie.

At the same time, my loner sensibility remains a part of who I am. The pattern is pretty clear: When I had the falling-out with STP after *Tiny Music*, I went off and did my first solo project, *12 Bar Blues*. When I later fell out with Velvet Revolver, the band I joined after STP, I went off and did my second solo project, *Happy in Galoshes*. Both projects brought me deep satisfaction. It was also a way to tell my bandmates, "Ciao, so long, *buenas noches*." But beyond my temporary anger, I needed some artistic time away from STP.

On *12 Bar*, I was reflecting on being alone, reflecting on how I had hurt Jannina. In a song called "The Date"—which I wrote, played all the instruments, recorded, and mixed in about an hour—I sang about how "she waits for a date and yet she knows that he's not coming." I was in a Lennon-circa-his-primal-scream-period phase. It wasn't about making beautiful music; it was just raw emotion. I was pleased, though, when Daniel Lanois called it the most beautiful of my songs.

Raw emotion drove a song like "Mockingbird Girl," which I had written when, for a short period, I was with a group called the Magnificent Bastards, a side project that allowed me to take new sorts of musical risks. The band was an excuse for one great song and a lot of broken needles. "Mockingbird Girl" concerns a friend who fell for a girl whom he couldn't quite grab hold of. It was used in a film called *Tank Girl* and, to my ears, has a George Martin Beatles sound.

While in the studio working on *12 Bar*, I happened to glance at the TV. The film *Barbarella* was on, and I found myself riveted. I wrote a song using that title. The lyrics are obscure, but reading them today, I see my desire for a strong, powerful woman to come along and cure me of everything. "You play the game," I wrote. "I'll masturbate and play a lullaby. You ran the race. I'll pay the miles. You sing the pin love fuzz and dance the musty queer. I'll stay at home 'cause I'm the mouse. So high that I can't fly . . ."

MUSICAL RISKS

I was really grateful—and honored—when Sheryl Crow came in and played on "Lady, Your Roof Brings Me Down."

When I wrote "Where's the Man," I was living alone in a rented apartment—split from Jannina—and filled with regret. "Where's your man, he's lost and gone again. What's your name? The name behind the shame."

I was awash in shame. I was still hooked on heroin. I wanted out but didn't know what that meant.

12 Bar Blues wasn't a hit by any means. It didn't sell anywhere near the numbers of STP, but it was critically acclaimed. I wasn't surprised because so much of it sounds like it's from outer space—my home address at the time. Talk Show, the band the other Pilots had formed with Ten Inch Men singer, Dave Coutts, suffered the same lack of success.

I was bummed but decided to tour anyway. I formed an all-male band called Scott Weiland and the Action Girls. When we played New York, I went downtown to score dope in my old Lower East Side stomping ground, but by then, unbeknownst to me, the game had changed. There were no more hassle-free easy-access drug sales. Walking out of one of those nasty tenements with a fresh purchase in my pocket, I was nailed by a couple of cops. The Atlantic Records publicist bailed me out. I was so sick that someone suggested I try what's called an overnight opiate detox. They put you under and you wake up feeling like you've been hit by a Mack truck. Problem was, the fuckers didn't give me enough to keep me under. I awoke in full withdrawal, shitting, puking, cramping, and screaming, "Help! Help!" A nurse came in and said nothing could be done until they got hold of the doctor. It took thirty minutes of agony before he got there.

I went back to L.A., where still another rehab awaited me.

"WANNA MAKE a ROCK RECORD?"

T HAT WAS THE QUESTION DEAN ASKED ME over the phone.
   "Not sure," I said. "What do you have in mind?"
   "A raw rock record. Nothing fancy. Just balls-out rock and roll. Back to basics."

   I liked the idea. I did not, however, like the absence of an apology from either Dean, Robert, or Eric for trashing me in public. I still harbored big-time resentments. But I was practical—as were they. If my solo project had gone through the roof, or if their Talk Show record had sold millions instead of thousands, we probably wouldn't be talking. But Dean did call with this idea that seemed pretty sound.

   "Besides," he said, "we're building a legacy. It's important we stay together and not let shit tear us apart."

   So we got together and started jamming. My plan to continue working alone was trumped by a chance to put out a strong STP record and make good money.

   The truth about working alone is this: Even during those periods when I was estranged from my bands, I often fell in with another collaborator. In that regard, no one has been closer to me than Doug Grean, soul brother to the bone. When I met him, I was in the process of putting together my recording studio and Doug had some equipment I could use. He presented himself as an engineer, and in that capacity we started working together.

Didn't take long before I saw that, more than an engineer, he was a superb guitarist, trained in the rich soil of New Orleans funk, capable of playing in any genre. Beyond playing, though, Doug proved to be an ace composer. In short order, we hit it off and became a team. Doug took on different instruments—various keyboards and the tricky lap-steel guitar—enlarging our musical palette. I also started toying with keyboards, although my contributions were mostly sounds and sprinkles in a Brian Eno–esque mode.

EVERYONE IS WRONG

Doug was an important contributor to the new STP album, which we would title *No. 4.*

All the songs were written together live. Brendan O'Brien, our brilliant longtime producer, urged us simply to put our hearts and souls on the line. What came out was, at least in my mind, a good record of generic rock. What kick-started things, though, was one single—"Sour Girl"—that turned into the biggest hit of STP's career. The fact that we created a far-out video to accompany the song didn't hurt. Since its release, everyone is convinced that it's about my romance with Mary. But everyone is wrong.

"Sour Girl" was written after the collapse of my relationship with Jannina. It's about her. "She was a sour girl the day she met me," I wrote. "She was a happy girl the day she left me . . . I was a superman, but looks are deceiving. The roller-coaster ride's a lonely one. I pay a ransom note to stop it from steaming."

The ransom note, of course, was the fortune our divorce was costing me. And the happy state, which I presumed to be Jannina's mood, was due to the fact that she had finally rid her life of a man who had never been faithful.

"I Got You" is another song that has me musing on Jannina and how, time and again, she tried to save me from myself. I wrote, "I got you, but it's the craving for the good life that sees me through troubled times, when the mind begins to wander to the spoon. And I got you because you're there to bend and nurture me through these troubled times."

"And I don't believe it," says a song called "Church on Tuesday," "is she really gone again?" It's Jannina who is gone, Jannina whom I have pushed away, Jannina's family who I visualize in church, praying for a man to honor their daughter in a way I never did.

When *No. 4* was finished, the logical move was to tour behind it and let our fans know STP was back and stronger than ever. The only problem, though, was that I was weaker than ever. I was still fucking with dope. I was in the midst of a firestorm romance with Mary. And, finally, I wasn't available to support the album because, when it came time to kick off the tour, I found myself heading for jail.

"*The*
PAINTED
CLOWN"

*—from "Lady, Your
Roof Brings Me Down"*

MY PLAN WAS ALWAYS TO AVOID JAIL. Rehab was my only hope. The court said so, and I knew so.

When I got to rehab, though, the emotional chemistry changed when a nurse slipped me a note that said, "Mary Forsberg is looking for you."

My heart started hammering, my pulse racing. Apparently Mary had been having drug problems of her own and wanted to join me at this recovery home. Part of me wanted her to check in. But a smarter part of me knew it was a terrible idea.

I told the people running the rehab not to admit her. Mary found another place to recover but left after a few days. A week later, on my birthday, she sent me a card. All it said was "Happy Birthday, Baby!" That's all it needed to say. It sent chills down my spine.

I wanted to see her, and after moving to a sober living house I sought her out. At the time she was living at Charlize Theron's place, which was under reconstruction. A few days later, I did what I had longed to do— move in with Mary. We were hopelessly in love.

Hopelessly.

A LITTLE WHILE LATER, we were living together in an apartment off the mid-city Miracle Mile in L.A. We were also doing coke together. This was before we were married and had kids. I was slipping on and off heroin when Mary and I went to a party where an old friend offered me a fix. I said yes. Mary was distressed; she begged me not to, but I couldn't be dissuaded.

"Well," Mary said, "if I can't stop you, I want to do it too. I want to know what it feels like. I want to know what *you* feel like when you do it."

"You once snorted it."

"But that didn't do anything. I want to shoot it."

"One time only," I said. "One time and that's it."

She agreed.

I prepared it. She tied off. After shooting her up, I watched her fall into an easy ecstasy.

Later she said, "I felt more peace than I've ever felt in my life."

She immediately knew why I did what I did.

My song "Bi-Polar Bear," released in 2002, centers on something I discovered about Mary and myself years earlier: bipolarity. Friends and colleagues had been saying that maybe my drug condition and her erratic behavior and uncontrollable moods were more than simple mood volatility. So we went to a psychiatrist who specialized in such evaluations. We both passed the test with flying colors. We were both bipolar bears. The lyrics say,

> So I'm halfway letting go again
> I'm halfway full on
> Left my meds on the sink today
> My head will be racing by lunchtime

The romance with Mary always felt like a footrace—her catching up with me, me catching up with her. We'd break up to make up and start all over again. She'd swear me off. I'd swear her off. But my need for her was as great as my need for beautifully destructive drugs. For months, we were happy together, protecting each other from the cruelty of a world that couldn't understand us. Only we understood each other. Then for months we would stay apart, realizing the futility of trying to forge two spirits moving in different directions.

A SONG I NEED TO WRITE:

It concerns a stripper I dated after I had broken up with Jannina and was on the outs with Mary. The moment I came home, this accommodating lady fell on her knees to pleasure me. A half hour later she was throwing plates at my head. I have the title—"Flame Thrower"—but the melody remains locked up somewhere in my imagination.

WHEN MARY AND I DID GET PAST THE FIGHTS and pledged to stay together, drugs were always in the mix. After her initial fix, it wasn't long before we were getting loaded all the time. Our atypical form of domestic bliss was interrupted when I was court-ordered to live in a sober living house. During the day, though, I'd leave the house to hang out with Mary so we could get high together.

HERE IS AN EXCERPT FROM MY JOURNAL that I wrote in that period:

As heated as the passion is between us—passion that borders on mutual obsession—we do everything together, and everything is an adventure. It's Bonnie and Clyde, rock and roll. Hell on Wheels. We know we're gonna crash,

but we keep on going. Get a place in Hollywood. Spanish Moroccan chic. Perfect
for who we think we are. We're off on a run of speedballs—heroin and coke—of
legendary proportions. Mary's new at it, but I've never seen anyone escalate to
such a high level in such a short period of time. Mary is my match, my equal, my
heart, my soul, my love, my drug. The run takes us from coast to coast, jet-setting
with her fashion friends in New York, hanging with movie stars in L.A. But what
goes up has to come down—and it does. Hard. After a while, we're the only ones
who think we're looking good and doing well. We can't keep appointments. We
go through hundreds of thousands of dollars. Our friends start questioning our
every move. Some friends walk away. We start questioning ourselves. It's alright
for me to despise myself, but I can't stand seeing Mary do that to herself.

SICK AND TIRED OF BEING SICK AND TIRED, I decided to kick once and for
all. The sober living house wasn't working, so I went to a doctor for pills.
He gave me the wrong medicine. The stuff he prescribed sent me into
an immediate and violent seizure. Chills, heat, sweat, shakes. I was puking
and shitting my brains out. I called Mary and said, "Take me to a hospital."

The hospital doctors tried overriding the bad pills with morphine
and liquid valium. My skin was crawling, my stomach rumbling; I couldn't
stop puking, shaking, and shitting. While the doctors frantically looked for
ways to keep me in one piece, Mary slipped out of my hospital room to the car,
where she shot speedballs. It was one of the craziest nights of our crazy life.

Next morning, when the nurse came into my room, she saw Mary
lying on top of me, both of us passed out from dope exhaustion. They put
us in wheelchairs and rolled us out. A counselor, who had treated Mary
and me, was standing there with her hands on her hips. She sighed and
said, "Mary and Scott, what in the world am I going to do with you two?"

The hospital called the head of the sober living house, who called the judge to report my deviant behavior. I was given a court date, and I was sentenced.

Mary and I, two junkies passed out on top of each other on a hospital bed.

Romantic, isn't it?

We may have been side by side in wheelchairs, but I was the one going to jail to get clean. Mary, at least for the time being, kept getting high. She found a friend and got fucked up.

I WANNA LEARN ALL,
EXPERIENCE ALL.
BLISS AND PAIN.
TRUTH FROM FRAUD.

"FALLING FURTHER

FURTHER

with a

FLAMING

HAND"

—*from "Pruno"*

THE JUDGE GAVE ME A YEAR, which was reduced to five and a half months. Fortunately, I avoided the downtown county jail and was put into a drug program that was run in a former Japanese internment camp in California. We slept in barracks rather than cells. We were put on work details, given no privileges to speak of, but were lucky enough to have therapy sessions. A twelve-step model, with which I was already familiar, was used. I understood the concept of admitting the unmanageability of my addiction, recognizing a higher power, and the necessity of turning my life over to that power, as opposed to my own broken-down willpower. I needed to surrender my willfulness, my ego, and my need for control. The question was: Could I?

I could get along with the other inmates. We were more afraid of the tough-ass counselors than we were of one another. The one thing we wanted to avoid was being sent to the Mainline—the general jail population. The counselors had the power to send you there in a heartbeat. They didn't need a reason. I worked hard not to give them a reason, and I succeeded.

Mary wrote me practically every day. Hers were letters of extreme passion and longing. I answered her with equally impassioned words of love. My loving mother wrote as well. So did my stepdad and even my blood father, Kent, but no one really knew what to say. The truth was that after fucking up countless times I had landed in jail.

The salvation was music. When Christmas 1999 came rolling around, I organized a musical program. In our singing group we had blacks, skinheads, and Latinos, but harmony ruled.

Inside jail, I felt okay. It was great being off drugs, exercising, participating in therapy, reading books, and putting together a choir. It was great being straight. My goal—as always—was to stay straight. My goal was to put the nightmare of opiates behind me. I had everything to live for. Mary and music were waiting for me.

What could go wrong?

I WANNA KNOW WHAT THE
RENT'S LIKE IN HEAVEN.
STILL WANNA KNOW
WHERE THE RIVER GOES...

Wedding dance to "At Last"

Mary envisioned this moment from the first day she met me.

POSITIVE
SOUL
REGENERATION

"Celebrate the immoral youth that wasted you
Peel the skin back from all the lies that blistered you"

— FROM "REGENERATION"

OUT OF JAIL, READY TO ROCK, ready to re-promote *No. 4*, I joined up with STP to relaunch the record. The campaign was twofold: First, Dean and I went around the country, playing acoustic versions of the songs for select radio stations. Second, the full band went on tour, co-headlining with the Red Hot Chili Peppers. I'd been a big fan of the band in their early days and was thrilled to be on a bill with them. Most of the reviewers thought that we dominated the shows. The Peppers weren't happy about those articles, but a little friendly competition among rock bands is good for the fans. Being that close to a group as powerful as the Peppers certainly brought out our best.

I MARRIED MARY FORSBERG IN 2000 at the Little Door restaurant in Los Angeles. Some 120 people attended. Because I was divorced, a Catholic priest wouldn't marry us, but a liberal rabbi, with deep respect for all loving theologies, officiated and suggested we write our own vows. I said that I had been in love before, but my heart was broken. I was married once before, and I thought I knew what love was about. But it was Mary who taught me the meaning of love, true love. I said that she was my soul mate, my everything.

To the WOMAN WHO I AM going TO SPEND
the rest of my life with...
To MARY WEILAND

Will you MARRY me MARY?

Yes ☒   NO ☐

COMMENTS: I PROMISE to love you with
all of my heart for the rest of my life. I will take care
of you forever no matter what. I will give you beautiful
healthy children. you will Always feel loved As long As I'm Alive.
I Love you more than anything, my beautiful husband.

It is officiAL. THIS IS A BiNDiNG
LegAL DOCUMENT, VALID IN ALL CiTiEs
iN ALL STATES iN EVERY country of the
WiDE, WiDE world.
SMALL (NOT Exclusive to this solar system) PRiNT
       (iN FACT this is All universe INclusive)

BRiDE   GROOM

X Mary FORSbERG   X S. Weiland
Mary H. FORSbERG   SCOTT R. WEILAND
AKA- mary Weiland

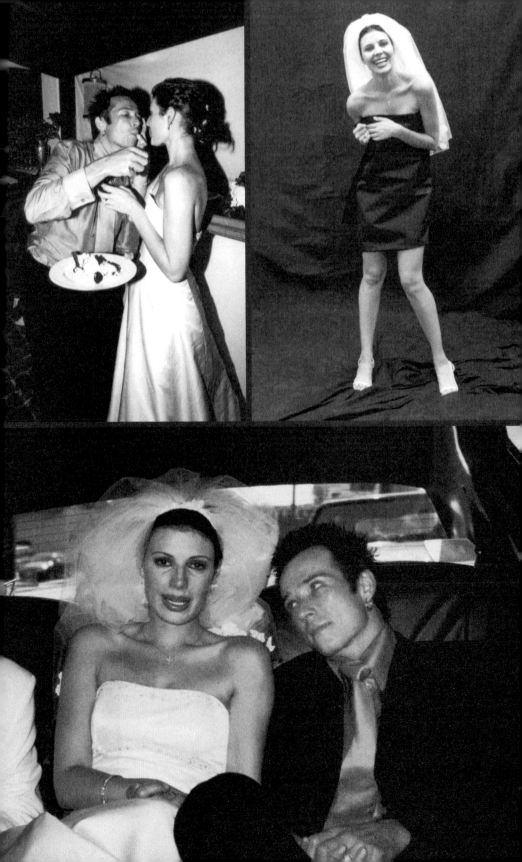

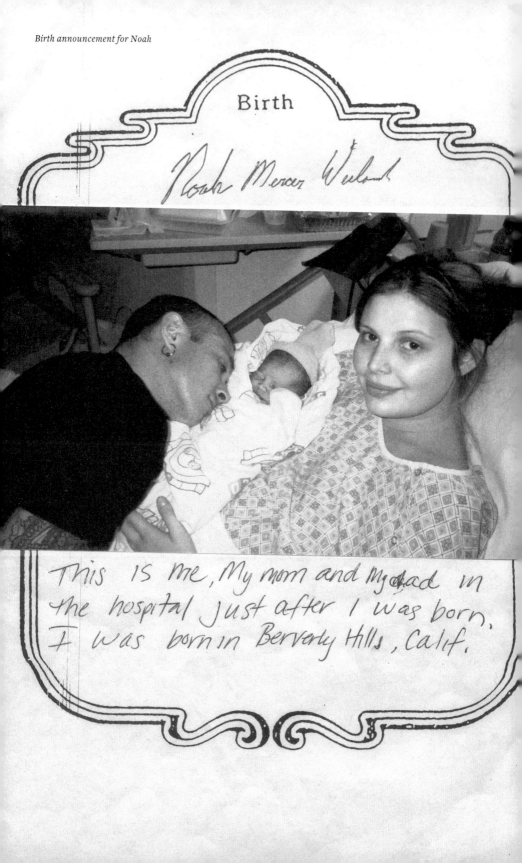

Birth

Noah Mercer Weiland

This is me, My mom and My dad in the hospital just after I was born. I was born in Berverly Hills, Calif.

NOAH

MARY WAS EIGHT MONTHS PREGNANT with our son, Noah. We were at the restaurant Sushi on Sunset in L.A. Mary and I got up and went to the unisex bathroom. As we went in, some frat guys followed us. We closed the door behind us. Impatient to use the bathroom, the guys loudly banged on the door. I went out to quiet them down. "Come on," I said, "show some respect." They called me a fag. I told them to get fucked. They came after me. One guy head-butted me. Hearing the ruckus, Mary emerged from the bathroom and punched my attacker full in the face.

MARY GAVE BIRTH TO OUR SON, NOAH, IN 2000. It was one of the most beautiful moments of my life. I had been clean for eighteen months, a minor miracle. The major miracle was Noah. When he made his grand entrance into the world, I was right there in the hospital room to greet him. My heart swelled. I've never experienced such joy. On the next Stone Temple Pilots record, *Shangri-La Dee Da*, I sang "A Song for Sleeping" for Noah:

Will you tell me the little things?

What does God look like?

And angels' wings?

I don't remember these things

So would you teach them to me?

For the moment

I'll watch you breathe

Me and Noah

With Usher and Clive Davis

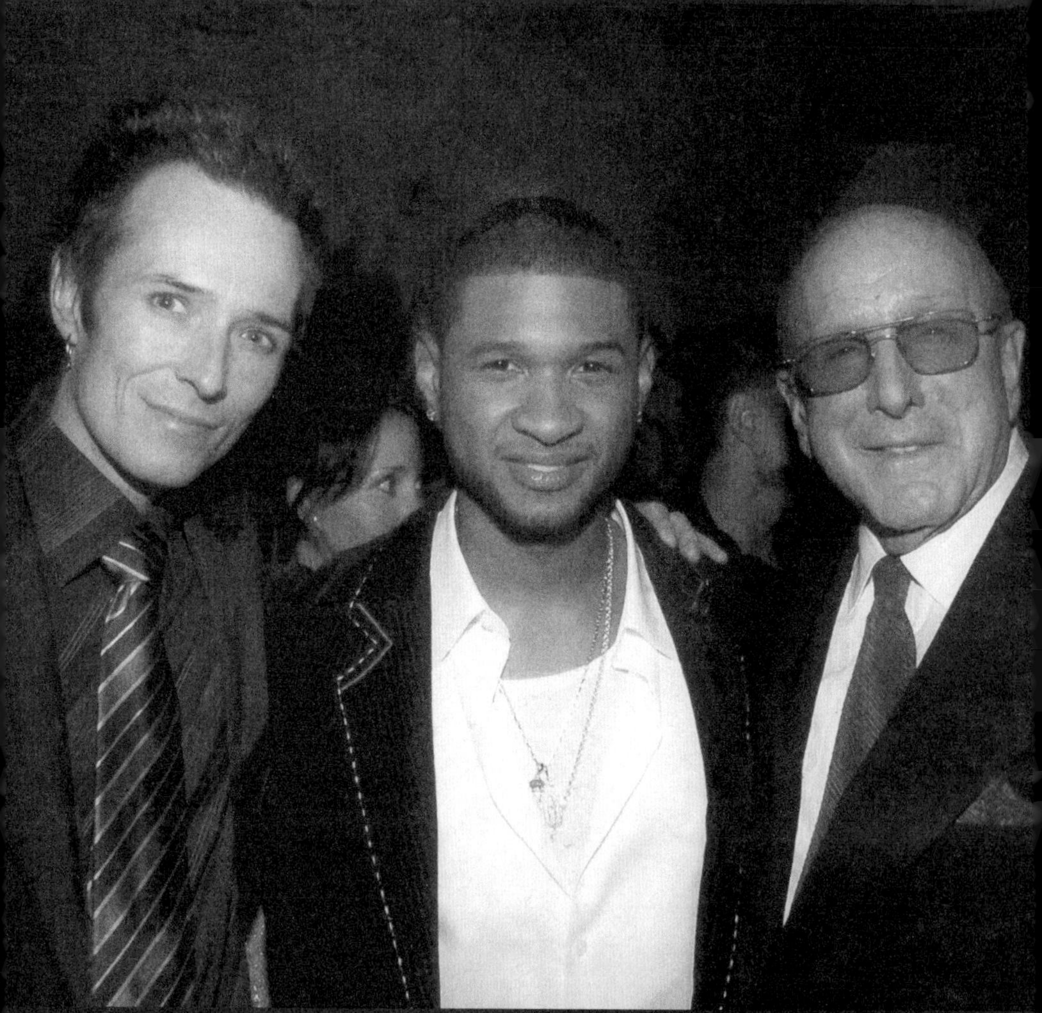

The
DEVIL'S
in the
SUN

Take a bath with consecrated water from the shrine
and wash away the mud of all the miles you left behind
Triplicates and wedding rings both lethal to obtain
So batten down the credit cards, the devil's in the den

—FROM "TRANSMISSIONS FROM
A LONELY ROOM"

N EW TUNES, NEW RECORDS, new marriage, new son.

By then, Doug Grean was my steady and stupendously creative sidekick. He helped me and the other Pilots put together a suite of songs that eventually became *Shangri-La Dee Da*. This time, as opposed to the more commercial approach of *No. 4*, the four of us agreed that we wanted to break on through the other side.

When we were done, the suits wanted us to put out, as the first single, a more pop-oriented song, "Days of the Week." Well, to satisfy our core following, we had always led off with a rock single. We wanted "Coma," a song that said, "Tar and feather hide your feelings, if you even know the meaning, your high road is overrated, you left your guru out there hangin'."

Well, the suits prevailed and we were left out there hangin' with "Days of the Week." Our fans were disappointed and our sales flagged. No matter, we hit the road again in support of this, STP's fifth studio record in less than ten years. If you throw in my *12 Bar Blues*, that makes six, a lot of music from someone with a screaming and demanding addiction.

Writing the music and lyrics for *Shangri-La Dee Da* was a continuation of my attempt to understand that addiction. The song "Dumb Love," for example, tells the story:

Alcohol, it's a lie, stimulate a needle in your eye
Let it bleed, blow your mind
Touched myself, nearly went blind
Couldn't find a way to live through the pain . . .
Couldn't get outta bed
Ten-ton bricks layin' on my head
Persecute the crucified
Kill a man for losing his mind
Couldn't find a way to live through the shame . . .

"Hello It's Late" has a Burt Bacharach vibe and is deeply sorrowful. My marriage to Mary was young but our fights felt old. It's a song about doubt and fear for the future. "It's just a game we used to play," I wrote, "and I didn't think we'd take it all the way. It kills me just because it can't be erased. We're married."

"Wonderful" has me dreaming about my death. In the next world, I envision Mary as my guide:

If I were to die this morning
Would you tell me things that you wouldn't have?
Would you be my navigator?
Would you take me to a place where we could hide?
. . . I wanna ask you to forgive me
I haven't been the best with all that I had
Wish I'd only laid beside you
I think I spread myself too thin

WHEN MARY'S DEPRESSION HIT HER HARD, she'd say that her "black clouds" had returned. During those times when we were able to comfort each other, our bond was beautiful. In that spirit, I wrote "Black Again" for Mary:

> *When you're fed up and lonely*
> *And nothing else seems to matter really*
> *I'll be waiting for you*
> *I'll be here to hold your hand*
> *When you're tired and lonely*
> *Hold your breath underwater*
> *And know you'll rise to the surface slowly*
> *Think of me as a ship that might hold you*
> *Carry you to the shore when you're tired and lonely*

The most distinctively non-love song on *Shangri-La Dee Da* was "Too Cool Queenie," written with Ms. Cobain in mind. Mary and I happened to run into her in New York at a time when she was feuding with members of Nirvana. In an offhand fashion, I told a fanciful version of the story of her and Kurt:

> *There was this girl who lived not too long ago*
> *As a matter of fact I think she lives still*
> *She knew she could do no wrong just singing those songs*
> *That we all knew*
> *She would always crash the party, it was no surprise, it was for her*
> *Too cool Queenie*

———————

There was this boy, he played in a rock 'n' roll band
And he wasn't half bad at saving the world
She said he could do no right, so he took his life
His story is true
. . . And now this girl, she got real famous
And she made lots of money and some of his too
But still she thinks she can do no wrong just playing those songs
She's all too cool

The sales for *Shangri-La Dee Da* weren't especially cool, and neither was the tour to support the record. However, the reviews were great. This was a new era when rock fans were going Napster. The whole band was partying hard, me included, but Dean was hiding that fact and blaming all mishaps on me. Meanwhile, I came down with a lung infection and was coughing like mad. At one point, I lost my voice. Onstage, whenever my voice failed, Dean looked over at me as if to say, "Why are you fucking up again?"

I quickly had my fill of his passive aggression.

"What's the deal?" I said, confronting him backstage.

"You sound like shit," he retorted.

"I sound like shit because my lungs are congested. What's the worst thing that happens to you—you get a little blister on your finger?"

"Fuck you."

"Fuck you!"

We were about to get physical when our sober coach—a man with a thankless task—stepped between us. There had been fights between Dean and Robert in the past—I remember them throwing chairs at each other—but Dean and I had never come to blows. This time we were inches away.

This time I also realized that I hadn't gotten past the built-up resentment of being publicly dissed during their press conference on the *Tiny* tour. This time I realized that, once again, I wanted to retreat and find my own way.

Shangri-La Dee Da, a title that flippantly referenced a place that was supposedly heaven on earth, turned hellacious in a hurry. Still, I think of it as our most adventurous work.

My magnificent daughter,
Lucy (or Louie!)

LUCY

A FTER THE SECOND BREAKUP OF STP, I went back out on junk. Understandably, Mary was disgusted with me. Mary was clean and, not only that, Mary was pregnant with our second child.

I desperately wanted to be clean and present for our daughter's birth. I went into rehab ahead of schedule so I could get out in time. But things got screwed up and the counselors were late letting me out of treatment. Mary also gave birth ten days early. I missed the birth by thirty seconds, and I'll regret it forever. But Lucy, beautiful Lucy, was in my arms that day, in the arms of her mother, Mary, in our arms forever.

That same year at Christmas we experienced a miracle. Compared to the dark spirits that haunted me during the reign of cocaine, this spirit of light came to our family as an absolute blessing and reminder of the power of faith.

My grammy, my mom's mom, was sick with an infection of the brain—encephalitis. Her memory was gone. She barely recognized any of us. On Christmas Eve she was released from the nursing home and came home with us. The doctors said her chances to recover were nil.

That night we put the kids to sleep, trusting that visions of sugarplums would dance in their heads. Santa Claus did his thing, and early in

---

the morning we gathered around the tree to open presents. Somewhere around eight a.m., Grammy came downstairs and began to call our names. She recognized every one of us—her husband, her daughter, her grandchildren, her great-grandchildren. She had perfect clarity, perfect recall. A nurse, whom I had hired to stay with her, said in all her professional life she had never witnessed this kind of recovery. Two days later, Grammy and Grandpa drove back home to Oceanside. Grammy was fine.

I learned that God and the angels of the Lord can turn around everything and revive life. Miracles happen. Of that I had no doubt. In some ways, my own nuclear family was a miracle.

It was 2002, and I seemed to have it all:

The woman I loved, the children I loved.

I was motivated to do everything I could to save the family, the marriage, the life I had long dreamed of.

I was determined.

I was strong.

I was committed.

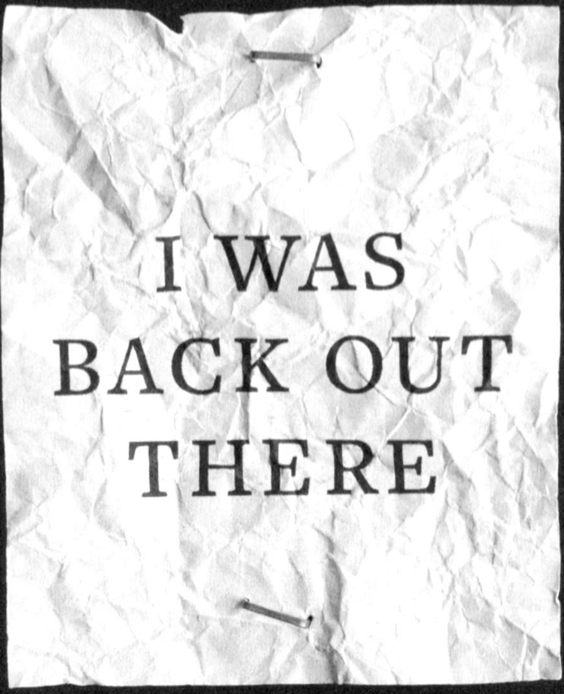
I WAS
BACK OUT
THERE

S LIPPING AND SLIDING, PEEPING AND HIDING.

Basically, the story was that Mary had cleaned up and I hadn't. I was strung out and fucked up. Mary wanted out of the marriage—the agony of our divorce went on for years—but Mary still took an interest in my career. Always has. Always will. Ka-ching. Ka-ching.

She said she'd been hanging with Susan McKagan, a former swimsuit supermodel and wife of Duff, the bass player with Guns N' Roses when the group was at its height. Susan told Mary that three guys from GNR—Duff on bass, Matt Sorum on drums, and Slash on guitar—had formed a band. Initially, Izzy Stradlin was in, but soon opted out. David Kushner from Wasted Youth took his place.

"Sounds like a lot of egos," I said. "Sounds like a lot of trouble."

"They put some songs on a CD that they want you to hear," Mary said. "They think you'll like what they're doing."

I didn't. It sounded like Bad Company–styled classic rock. And I never liked Bad Company. But being a nice guy, I said, "There's some stuff that's okay, but just send me another disc when you have a few new songs."

A week or so later, another CD arrived with songs custom-designed for me. The tunes had STP written all over them.

Duff called and said, "Hey, man, just drop by the studio." I knew Duff from the gym, and I said I'd try. I still wasn't sure whether I wanted to hook up with these guys.

"Look, Scott," Duff said, "there's also soundtrack stuff we've been asked to do. And the money's great."

STREET GANG

The money attracted me. My managers, pushing me to join this band, said, "They're going to cover Pink Floyd's 'Money' for a new movie called *The Italian Job*. And then Ang Lee wants songs for his remake of *The Hulk*. This is going to be a hot band. Just give it a chance."

I reluctantly agreed. The idea was just to jam. Couldn't hurt to see if there was any chemistry. Meanwhile, I was still hurting chemically. I was still shooting dope. That's the reason I showed up many hours late.

When I arrived, I was shocked. The guys had set up a major industry event. All sorts of music execs were there. It was being billed as an announcement of "Guns N' Roses with Scott Weiland" and made to look like a done deal, not just a casual jam. I was confused, and, because of my drug habit, I was also a wreck. But what the fuck, I was there and might as well sing.

We sang two songs—"Set Me Free" for *The Hulk* and the cover of "Money." I was blown away by the powerful chemistry between us. So was everyone else. These guys attacked rock and roll like a street gang. I liked their ferocity and balls-out commitment. Besides, looking over and seeing Slash playing beside me—Slash, who'd been an idol of mine back

in the eighties—was a thrill. I knew Dave Kushner from the Electric Love
Hogs, an underground rock band. Back in the day, STP had aspired to be
on the Love Hogs level. I remember seeing them at English Acid, a hip
spot in West Hollywood. I also knew Matt Sorum from rehab; he and I
had been in together.

Fact is, I had a lot in common with these guys. We'd been down the
dark alleys, gotten mugged, stumbled, fell, and got back up. When I hooked
up with them, they were looking good. Through martial arts, Duff had put
together eight years of sobriety. Matt had six years. And Dave had over a
dozen years. When they saw my strung-out condition, they vowed to do
everything in their power to help.

WIND

and

ROCK

I WENT BACK TO REHAB but rehab didn't work. That's when Duff started talking about his trainer in Lake Chelan, Washington State. "Bring your detox meds and come up there with me," Duff offered. "You'll meet my martial arts master, one guy who can really help you."

His help came quickly and powerfully. His name is Sifu Joseph Simonet, and he's a master of six different martial arts forms. I planned to stay a month but stayed for three. At his Wind and Rock training facility, I also worked with his associate and fiancée at the time, Addy Hernandez, a kickboxer and holder of a black belt in kenpo karate. Sifu Simonet comes from a kung fu background in addition to the art form of Pentjak Silat Tongkat Serak. He created his own form called Key Fighting Concepts and, from day one, I related to his energy. He's a deeply wise man with a bit of a temper and a flair for martial arts instruction and philosophical riffing.

"My art form never stops evolving," he likes to say. "I can never repeat myself because the past is gone and the present is ever new, ever changing."

With intense daily training, I learned to channel my aggression, confusion, fear, and athleticism in positive directions. The rigorous routine allowed me to wean myself off opiates. The setting also helped. Lake Chelan Valley sits in the center of the magnificent North Cascades National Forest. The lake is a breathtakingly beautiful fifty-mile, glacier-fed body of crystal-clean water. Nature is untamed. Bears and wild goats roam the mountains. I fell in love with the area and decided to buy land there and, in time, build a cabin in the woods.

Back in Los Angeles, I hooked up with Benny "the Jet" Urquidez, a five-time world-champion kickboxer. Benny boasts that he has never been defeated, and when you train with him, you don't doubt it. He was my instructor for eighteen months after I returned from Lake Chelan. This was a difficult period—around 2006—because Mary and I were still doing a death dance around our marriage. I'd walk into Benny's dojo—his karate gym—and right away Benny could read my mind.

"You're depressed," he'd say. "The energy between you and your wife has turned especially toxic this week."

"How do you know that?"

"I'm looking in your eyes—that's how."

Then Benny would start to explain the concept of being "glazed." He said that obviously anyone can incur physical injury. But once you're glazed, you're mentally and spiritually protected from harm. The glaze resists negative thoughts. Of course, like everyone, you will be affected by external circumstances, feelings, and moods, but the impact will be minimal because of the strength of your spiritual and mental muscles.

Glazed.

Ready to walk back into the world a whole man, ready to accept the world on its own terms.

Ready to get out there, join up with a balls-out rock band, and reinvent myself as a singer and artist.

It was going to work.

It had to work.

It did.

And then it didn't.

"JOURNAL *of* MEMORIES, FEELING LONELY CAN'T BREATHE"

—*from "Fall to Pieces"*

B ACK IN 2003, after I joined Velvet Revolver and got straight, I wrote all the lyrics and all of the melodies for our first album, *Contraband*, which wound up selling over four million copies. The big hit was "Fall to Pieces." Duff and I wrote it at Lavish, the studio I built in Burbank. It was built on a riff by Slash, and somehow in the middle of the night we turned it into a song about coming to terms—or not coming to terms—with my heroin addiction. It was also about my relationship with Mary, and how it was falling apart. When Mary wrote her memoir last year, she titled it *Fall to Pieces*. In the song, I sang . . .

> *All the years I've tried*
> *With more to go*
> *Will the memories die?*
> *I'm waiting*
> *Will I find you?*
> *Can I find you?*
> *We're falling down*
> *I'm falling*

WE WENT ON THE ROAD for two years, toured the world, and established ourselves as a premier rock band. Velvet Revolver was a powerful force. There was so much energy on that stage that at times it felt absolutely combustible. Anything could happen at any time. We were a bunch of renegades held together by a rough passion that none of us completely understood. We were dangerous. We were on a runaway train, and audiences were drawn to our breakneck speed.

I liked our first record but can't call it the music of my soul. There was a certain commercial calculation behind it. We wanted hits; we wanted to prove that, independent of Guns N' Roses and STP, we could make a big splash. And we did. My fellow STPers—Robert, Dean, and Eric—tried a number of musical configurations without me, but none of them were successful. I wished them well, but I have to confess that, as a competitive guy, I wasn't displeased to be in a new band that fans were flocking to see.

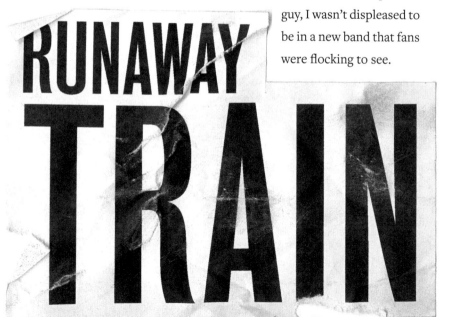

W HERE DOES IT COME FROM? WHAT IS IT?
I'm a tenacious drug addict. I give it up and I don't give it up. I put it down and I pick it up.

But I'm also a tenacious recoverer. I never quit trying to quit. That counts for something.

In the middle of all this, I'm a tenacious writer and performer. I need to compose; I need to sing; I need the feedback from real people. I'm tenacious not only about making art, but I also refuse to abandon my career.

I tenaciously cling to the notion that demonic forces are at work when we surrender our will to the world of drugs. I especially think that's true of cocaine. Cocaine—especially cooked-up, freebase crack cocaine—is downright evil.

I've had a series of cocaine encounters that have frightened me to death. At certain times, I've had to go back to my Catholic roots and recite prayers similar to those used by exorcists. But the negative forces were so powerful that I was unable to speak the holy words.

This has happened twice. The first time was in the late nineties; the second when I relapsed while playing with Velvet Revolver. In both instances, the dark presences made themselves known physically. There was stomping; there were actual forms facing me, the faces of skeletons. Otis, my golden retriever, bolted the room. He experienced what I experienced, saw what I saw, feared what I feared. I ran to the bathroom, locked myself inside, looked under the door and saw feet, saw shoes, heard voices, shook, shivered, prayed, tried to breathe, waited until the feet walked away and the noise stopped. I thought about what is perhaps the biggest question of man—is there life beyond this mortal coil?—and knew then that the answer is yes.

My belief is that the coke I was ingesting activated a paranormal force. That force once took the form of a minitornado, a whirlwind of tremendous energy that came after me and smashed against the side of the house, doing tangible damage.

Heroin is obviously intoxicating. Heroin kills all pain. Heroin kills the heroin addict. In my 1965 Ford Mustang, I'd drive to my heroin dealer, fix, and float out on a cloud. I'd float over Silver Lake Boulevard like the Goodyear blimp floating over the Rose Bowl on New Year's Day. The heroin high is the jet stream without turbulence—that is, until the jet explodes and crashes into the sea. The coke high, while wildly stimulating, is a roller-coaster ride through hell.

"I WANNA
KNOW WHY
YOU HAVE
TO GO"

—*from "The Man I
Didn't Know"*

AS MY LIFE WENT ON, my dad seemed to grow even more distant. As I was successful with music and unsuccessful with treating my addictions, I couldn't connect with my father. He would disappear for long periods of time, not answer my calls, ignore my attempts to get closer to him. That changed in 2003, though, when during a rehab stay he accepted my invitation to attend family week. That meant the world to me. He participated in therapy sessions and, for the first time, he appeared vulnerable and willing to listen to my confused feelings about him. After several heart-to-heart talks, he turned to me and said, "You know, Scott, as a father, I've failed you. So instead of trying to be a father, why don't I just try and be your friend. I think I can do that."

I was more than willing. Once out of rehab, I decided to have a weeklong Christmas celebration in my log house in the woods above Lake Chelan in Washington State. It was a male-bonding, multigenerational affair. I had my son, Noah; my dad, Kent; my brother, Michael; and my half brothers Seth and Matt, the boys Kent had with Martha. We bonded like a real family, riding snowmobiles, decorating the Christmas tree, exchanging presents, telling stories, and singing songs before the roaring fire. At night the winter sky was alight with a million stars. By day the world was a frozen wonderland. Michael seemed at peace. So did my dad. My son stayed by my side. I grew closer to Matt and Seth. It was beautiful.

And then it was over.

Michael went back into his dark world. My dad asked if his son Matt could work as my assistant. I agreed, but Matt, understandably, didn't love the job and never took it seriously. I had to let him go. I don't think that helped my relationship with my father. I called him, but he never called back. Months passed. Once again he disappeared. When he did call, he reached out to Mary when he heard that she and I were divorcing. He felt obliged to comfort her, not me.

Christmas time in Colorado at Mom and Dad's. Noah and Lucy's first snowman.

DO'S AND DON'T'S

========

Do love horses on trails.
Don't like motorcycles on the L.A. Fwy.

Do love escargot (since I was five).
Don't like fast food.

Do love winter and snow.
Don't like hot winter days.

Do love the mountains.
Don't like pretentious cities.

Do love an open heart.
Don't like dating.

Do love good sheets and a nicer hotel room.
Don't love to tour too long.

Do love our president.
Don't love a certain former governor of Alaska—
who does anymore?

Do like dressing well, as if you haven't put
any effort into it.
Don't like men that dress like cads.

========

Michael, in light, brighter days.
I miss those days.

The

DAY WE
LOST OUR
LIVES

I N 2007, I WAS AT HOME WITH THE KIDS. Mary was at Sundance, throwing parties for stars and socialites. The call came early in the day. It was a female friend of Michael's. She could hardly talk.

"Scott . . . Scott . . . oh my God . . ." she said. "I don't know how to say this. I'm at Michael's apartment and he's . . . he's gone."

"What do you mean 'gone'?" I asked.

"Michael's dead, Scott. He's dead. I don't know what to do . . . you've gotta come over here to identify his body. You're next of kin."

I went cold.

Seconds later, a burning hot sweat broke over me. I felt the vile, sour taste of vomit in my throat. From the pit of my soul, the same soul that was entwined with Michael's, this guttural wail . . . "No! No! No! No!"

The first thing I did was go to the liquor cabinet, fill a glass with whiskey, and drink it down. As an ex-junkie, my animal sense kicked in. I put on my emotional armor. I left the kids with the nanny and took off for Michael's apartment in Silver Lake.

While driving over, my head flooded with memories. I remembered as kids how Michael believed in Santa and Santa's elves. I'd dress up as an elf and run around the woods in back of our house. Then my parents, willing accomplices, would tell Michael to go look. He was completely fooled. Up to his early twenties, he still thought it was real, until it was casually mentioned one year over Christmas dinner. My brother had a delicate yet very old soul.

Only a month ago Michael had been happy for the first time in years. He was off dope, off crack. It felt like all our past troubles were behind us. He and his wife were on good terms and he was about to be granted visitation rights to his wonderful little girls.

Then his mirror image of himself snapped. For all the love in Michael's heart for his family and friends, he had none for himself. He weighed 180 pounds, but had only ten pounds of faith in himself. Maybe that's why they say that when you die, your shell loses ten pounds.

At some point during the drive over, I called Mary. She started wailing. This was unbelievably tragic, unbelievably sad. Out of instinct, I called Benny "the Jet" Urquidez, my sensei.

"What!" he screamed. "I lost my sister today!"

The ruthless law of mortality.

The horrible reality hit me between the eyes when I arrived at Michael's apartment. The police were there along with some of his friends. The place was chaos—piles of dirty dishes, broken plates, dust, the stink of filthy clothes, the smell of death. I walked to Michael's bed. He was stretched out; he seemed comfortable; his eyes were closed. It looked like him but it didn't *feel* like him.

A note was taped to his refrigerator, referring to his little girls: "Live for Sophia and Claudette." Was it a suicide note, or was it written in an inspired moment to remind himself of what he had to live for? I'll never know.

His heart gave out. Drugs, sure, but Michael died of a broken heart. That day a big part of me died as well.

Later we learned that it was cardiomyopathy, a disease of the heart muscle that four years earlier had been diagnosed by Dr. Drew Pinsky for me, not Michael, when I was in the throes of heroin detox.

Why Michael and not me?

Why was I always able to pick myself up off the ground and muddle through? Why didn't Michael have that ability?

There's a line in a Nirvana song that goes, "I miss the comfort of being sad."

That was Michael, but never me. Yet now I do feel that comfort of being sad. I miss the comfort of feeling anything.

Emptiness.

Loss.

A brother gone.

All this happened when we were making the second Velvet Revolver record, *Libertad*.

The brother of Matt Sorum, the Velvet Revolver drummer, also died during that same period.

We were left alone, haunted by questions of what we might have done, what we could have done, what we didn't do.

In a song on that record called "For a Brother" I wrote:

―――――――――

Could and should have been
And didn't
I've given up my hand for a brother
Given up a hand for free
I've risen and forgiven and I've pardoned
But you set yourself free

That word—freedom, *libertad*.
Another song on *Libertad*, "The Last Fight":

Break the chains of featherweights and giants
With disdain for everlasting lives!
They'll refrain when we spit out the fire
And start living

IN THE WAKE OF MICHAEL'S TRAGIC DEATH, things got worse with me and Mary. We started binge drinking. Our nanny would watch the kids; we'd go out for dinner, get plastered, and come home and have great sex. There were other times, however, when Mary showed no interest in drinking and sex at all. I could never tell. It was always a flip of a coin. Her mood swings, combined with my mood swings, could flip us in any direction. For *Libertad*, I wrote a song I couldn't call anything but "Mary, Mary."

Mary, Mary by my side
Atomic love the kind you cannot buy
Black boots, strong legs, got style
My baby knows the walk, you see her come from miles

———————————

Modern lover, modern kind

When we close the door, we're never out of time

Mary, Mary on my mind

. . . want to find out what you're saying

Want to play the games you're playing

Michael, alone

Michael with
his wife

Me and Michael

The
SMOKING
GUN

I WAS RUNNING WILD during the second Velvet Revolver tour. At the beginning of the tour, I was okay, but then a single line of coke in England did the trick. I snorted it. And soon the demons were back. Thus began another decline. That was 2007.

With my "Mary, Mary" obsession pulling me apart, and the grief from losing my brother breaking my heart, this little line of cocaine looked good. For me it was the same as stepping in quicksand. Before long, I was smoking the shit. After years of not doing street drugs—of not doing *any* kind of drugs—I was out there again, going to dangerous places to buy substances. All this was done in secret; the other guys in Velvet Revolver—all of whom except one, by the way, had suffered their own slips since the band formed—didn't know I was using.

Only my manager, Dana Dufine, knew of my decision to go into rehab. I had to. I couldn't live with myself; couldn't stomach the cold fact that I was back on the fuckin' pipe, doing what I had sworn I would never do again. When I told the guys that we'd have to miss a couple of gigs because I needed treatment, their reaction shocked me. They told me I'd have to pay them for those cancellations—in full. I reminded some of them that when they had relapsed and needed rehab, I had supported them completely. It made no difference to them. They wanted compensation from me, but this time, no deal. Fuck me once, shame me twice . . . well, just fuck off.

There had been other Velvet Revolver problems. Slash's wife, Perla, had inserted herself into the band business to the point of participating in band meetings. Beyond that, Velvet Revolver was essentially a manufactured product. For all our hits—"Fall to Pieces," "Slither," "Set Me Free"—we came together out of necessity, not artistic purpose.

The breaking point came when, after the tour for *Libertad* started up again, Matt wrote scathing things about me on the Internet. Our fragile brotherhood was permanently smashed. From a stage in England I told the crowd—along with my fellow bandmates—that they were witnessing a special event, Velvet Revolver's last tour. It didn't matter that Velvet Revolver had sold some five or six million records. I was out.

PARISIAN NIGHTMARE

I NEEDED TO GET AWAY. I had traveled my entire adult life, but always with an entourage—assistants, tour managers, security. My life was driving me crazy, and I needed time alone.

My idea was simple: go to Paris, book a room in Montmartre, my favorite part of the city, and chill. Write a little. Read a little. Relax for a week or two, hanging out in the bistros and soaking in the arty European vibe. I saw Paris as a city of quietude, beauty, and peace. It was the last place on earth I anticipated violence.

On the flight over, I remembered two violent encounters that had nearly done me in during the years when I was running the streets. In 1997, I was attacked at a downtown L.A. crack house by a crazy man with a homemade prison-style shank that struck me in the breastbone and fortunately broke off. A year later, during an STP tour, I was assaulted in Washington, D.C., when I tried to buy drugs in the projects. Again, I was lucky to have avoided serious injury. But that was all behind me. Paris was where I could chill out and find shelter from the emotional storms.

I arrived in early December. The hotel was cool; the nights were cold; and my head started to clear. I went down to Pigalle, with its tourist traps and fake "live" sex shows, and just wandered around. I was feeling free. Dressed in jeans, a T-shirt, and a plain North Face jacket, I was just another guy, not a rock star. I was walking through a park, thinking how great it was to be far away, when three guys approached me—one white, two black.

"We know about a party not far from here," they said. "You interested?"

They spoke in accents. The black dudes said they were Nigerian; the white guy was from Morocco.

"Sure," I said, thinking there might be weed or hash at the party.

"There are pretty girls too," they said. "Our car is right around the corner."

They seemed friendly enough, and I sensed no danger. Turned out, though, that the car wasn't around the corner. It was several miles away. Didn't matter. The night was invigorating. I was ready to go.

Once we got in the car and started driving to the party, the guys said they were Muslims.

"Fine," I said. "I respect Islam. I respect all the religions."

"I respect Hitler," said the black guy sitting next to me.

"Hitler!" I said. "How can you respect Hitler when he saw blacks as inferior? Hitler believed in the master white Aryan race. What's to respect about Hitler?"

"He got done what needed to get done."

"By creating the Holocaust?"

"Some people don't believe the Holocaust ever happened."

"Some people are crazy. The Holocaust is historical fact."

"I'm not at all sure."

Suddenly I wasn't sure what was happening. Obviously the party wasn't close by, because we had entered a freeway. When I asked where we were going, I got no answers, only sneers. Finally, after twenty minutes, we pulled off the freeway into a housing tract. The Moroccan, who was behind the wheel, kept turning in circles and doing donuts. He was intent on making me lose my bearings, an easy enough task.

"Where are we? What are you guys doing?" I asked.

When I got no answers, I knew I was in trouble. At that moment, as we turned up a dirt road, all my survival instincts kicked in. I opened the door and jumped out of the moving car.

Car screeched to the halt. The white guy came after me, chasing me at full speed. He caught me. We locked arms. I blocked his kicks. When

GOING FOR MY NUTS

he head-butted me, his forehead caught my open mouth. My tooth cut his skin and blood gushed out. My front tooth cracked in half. He was taken aback.

For all the fear coursing through me—fear of being murdered in cold blood—I was somehow able to hang on to a degree of control. I knew that if I panicked, it would also make things worse. Before I could put together a plan, though, the black guys were kicking me to the ground. One had a pair of pliers and was going for my nuts. I squirmed away and threw a wild elbow that—thank God—caught one of them square in the face.

The other grabbed my jacket that, because it was a slippery fabric and loose on my body, came sliding off me. The guy wound up holding the jacket, not me, and I took off.

I ran like the wind. I ran through the snow. When one of my shoes came off, I kept running. I jumped over a hedgerow and rolled down an embankment. Ran even harder until I found myself in a wooded area. My head was filled with one thought and one thought only: "*I'm not going to die here! I'm not going to die here!*" I hid under some leaves for thirty, forty minutes. I was freezing, wearing nothing but a T-shirt, jeans, and one shoe. When I thought it was safe to come out of hiding, I walked out of the woods where I found a neighborhood of small homes. I looked for one that had Christmas lights.

Knocked on the door.

Man answered. He looked me over. I was bruised, my T-shirt torn and covered with blood, my hair matted with twigs and leaves.

"I don't know French," I tried to say in French.

"I don't know English," he tried to say in English.

He called his daughter, who came downstairs. She knew English. I told her that I had been beaten, my passport and wallet, with eight hundred dollars, had been stolen, and I needed a ride back to my hotel. She believed me. She, her father, and her father's brother put me in their car and drove me to the hotel. I convinced the hotel manager to give them fifty euros for their trouble and thanked them profusely.

The next day I went to the American embassy for a temporary passport, the police station to file a report, and American Express to get some money.

——————

"After all you've gone through," my manager asked me over the transatlantic phone, "are you coming home?"

"No," I said. "I'm staying in Paris another four days. Then I'm going to Rome for a week."

When I finally did get home, I had my teeth reconstructed.

I still love Paris.

My fortieth birthday. A seventies roller-disco party. It turned out to be the last night of our marriage.

SHOES

of a

DARK

CLOWN

Marsey won't because she don't
and little Mary's crying
So what is a boy to do, wouldn't you
Mary's won't because she don't
and Mary keeps on crying
While promises break in two
And so do you

—SUNG TO THE MELODY OF "MAIRZY DOATS AND
DOZY DOATS AND LIDDLE LAMZY DIVEY"

T HE GREATER MY NEED FOR MARY, the greater her desire to dump me. More and more, she was expressing her loss of interest in me. All that was understandable. How many times can you put up with a man who moves in and out of rehab through a revolving door that never seems to stop? Mary had her own mental health to protect. I understood. Accepting the fact that she wanted to end our marriage was excruciatingly painful, but I had no choice.

So we separated. I moved out of our house with a pool into the Oakwood Apartments, temporary corporate housing, the same place Rick "Super Freak" James was staying. Mary lived her life, I lived mine. It went well for a period, but then Mary's dark clouds returned.

When she found out that, after our breakup, I had begun dating another woman, she fell into a crazed fury. Even though she was the one who had ended our relationship, the discovery of my involvement with someone else sent her into an altered state.

At the time, I was living at my own pad, but Mary wanted me back. I said okay. She went with me to pick up a moving truck to haul my stuff. On the way over, while I was driving, she kicked me in the face, screaming about this "other woman." She was so out of control that, to protect our two children, I took them to a hotel, where I booked a two-room suite.

Mary showed up at the hotel wearing a dress that she had cut up with scissors. I had to marvel at how she was totally aware and yet totally out

———————

of control at the same time. She took an entire handful of meds and washed them down with booze from the minibar. She drank until she passed out. I checked on her every few minutes to make sure she was breathing. She was, but she was also out cold.

I quickly came up with a plan. My manager, Dana, then a close friend of Mary's, agreed to take the kids that night. My mom agreed to fly in the next day.

When, in her semiconscious state, Mary heard the plan, she started yelling, "You're not taking the kids to Dana's today! And your mom's not going to take care of them tomorrow!"

I realized that Mom and Mary had a tenuous relationship, but, when it came to my kids, there was no one I trusted more than my mother. I had to stick with my plan. Mary's reaction was so violent—she started breaking dishes and mirrors—that I was frightened for our kids and called security. Mary was arrested and taken to a police station in Burbank. When she was released, she returned to the house, pulled all my clothes out of my closet, threw them into the driveway, drenched them in lighter fluid, and dropped a lit match. Eighty thousand dollars' worth of clothing up in flames. Mary was arrested again.

When Mary came back home, Mom had arrived and things had settled down—or so it seemed. Mary was interviewed by Child Protection Services—in fact we all were. She was ordered to a psychiatric hospital for evaluation. She agreed to go, but only if I took her. At this point I was afraid of and for Mary.

Then Mary suddenly changed her mind. She wouldn't go. To keep me from leaving the house for a rehearsal, she blocked my car with hers.

I jumped over the fence and managed to get to my rehearsal. While I was gone, Mary got crazier, so crazy, in fact, that my mother took the kids into the master bedroom, locking the door behind her. Mary started screaming, "I'm leaving and taking my kids with me!" When Mary began kicking down the door, Mom opened it and tried to calm her down. That's when Mary went for her children; my mother stopped her, but, in doing so, Mary grabbed Mom by the neck, where Mom had recently had surgery. My mother told Noah to call 911. The cops arrived and, once again, Mary was ordered to check into an inpatient psych ward.

The next day Dana and I drove Mary to the hospital, but she wouldn't leave the car. Six nurses came out to try to convince her. Mary wouldn't budge. We took her to a bar, hoping liquid courage would help her see the light. She finally acquiesced to our pleading and signed herself into the hospital. Before Mary let us leave, though, she insisted that she needed stronger medication. A doctor agreed to give her a shot of Ativan. Still ranting, Mary was put in a ward for a seventy-two-hour period of observation. I don't know how, but two hours later she talked the hospital into releasing her. Mary signed herself out and came home, sicker than ever.

The drama went on for many months.

Finally, Mary went back on her meds regimen and found a modicum of stability. In recent times, that stability has deepened. Thank God. Her ongoing recovery has been a blessing for her, for me, and especially for our precious children.

I carry a tattoo of Mary on my arm that I wear like a badge, a jewel, a wound, a way to remind myself that love and pain, like blood and ink, swim in the same sea.

"Our Movie:"

Like a Jean Harlow picture
I look at you through the screen that divides us
I'm aware of the touch of your arms
I'm part of the sofa divider
I respect your space, enjoy your good taste
Yet I'm only one of the pieces that's in it
More, more, more, you're never finished
September, October, November, fall
December, January, February, snow
March, April, May, spring showers bear flowers
June, July, 4th of July, independence, here we go
But so long, Mr. August, it's been a wonderful show

CLEANING
JIMMY
CHOOS
with
HOLY
WATER

A FTER LEAVING VELVET REVOLVER, three significant things happened in my life: I began finalizing my divorce from Mary; I released a solo project that I'd been working on for years; and I rejoined my fellow Pilots for a new STP tour and record. I see these as positive developments.

The solo project—*Happy in Galoshes*, a two-disc collection that came out in 2008—was cathartic. I toured behind it with a band of avant-garde virtuosos called Scott Weiland and the Saffron Salvo.

Happy represents a great deal of work that I did with my friend Doug Grean, who also contributed greatly to my sanity. He was there through so much of the madness with Mary: He delivered and picked me up from rehab countless times; he put up with my unpredictability and cleaned up my messes; he understood me on the deepest and most compassionate level. I owe Doug a great deal.

I'm not one for idealization or sentimentalization, but *Happy in Galoshes*, at least in part, looks back on my life, like this memoir, with a degree of nostalgia. When it rained in Cleveland, I put on galoshes and went outside to play. I was certainly happy and, as a young child, carefree.

In the song "Missing Cleveland"—a key moment in the record—I reflect on that childhood with longing even as I remember the good times with Mary, when we'd put on our best outfits and go out to hip restaurants and people-watch:

You were dressed up at the ball
They expected us to fall
From the heavens its Lunar 7
They were monkeys all of them
Entertaining so we stayed
Wondering whether it's all or never

There are songs about my dad and my brother on *Happy in Galoshes*, but Mary is still the central character. I know that the great Italian poet Dante never got beyond his obsession with Beatrice, the woman-child of his dreams, and even put her in the center of his trip to paradise and vision of God. I'm not Dante, but I know, in my own small way, that my songs are hopelessly entangled with my obsession with Mary. She's at the center of the tune "She Sold Her System," a metaphor for my belief that she lost her passion for me. I see my passion for her as a force that never stops. I'm forever chasing her. "When in space on the hamster wheel," I sing, "will we ever win the saving race? And it's just too close to call while all the numbers crunch inside your head."

In "Pictures and Computers (I'm Not Superman)," I'm still trying to process the anger and pain I feel for Mary, the confusion, the bundle of contradictions that I carry around inside my head:

When I'm alone the world's at bay
Keeping them still as I slip away
But I'm not Superman and I'm not everyman
Have I done the best that I can to generate
'Cause I still hate
To revel around and terrorize or sympathize or populate
'Cause I'm just everyman who once was a stronger man
Who let the queen of his land burn off his cape
Now he just waits
Oh, let me be, you take a step and squash on everything
Your holy water won't clean those Jimmy Choos
You wear those shoes and then you run around all night

Guilt is there. My guilt about Michael, about Mary, about Jannina. "Big Black Monster" is a tune I wrote and recorded for *Happy in Galoshes* because it reminded me of how I had broken my first wife's heart. I'd tell Jannina, "Honey, I'm going out for a pack of cigarettes. Be back in fifteen minutes," then five days later would return home after staying in some low-rent hotel where I shot up coke and heroin.

Did you hear the monster come out?

He came a-crashin' in

Did you feel the monster come out?

You're crashin'

You're crashin'

But if anything summarizes the dance I've danced with women, it's "Tangle with Your Mind." I wrote this at a time when I was convinced that Mary had someone else. The telltale signs were too obvious to ignore. Mary, though, always felt that, when it came to mind games, she had the upper mind. She could outthink and outmaneuver me. She might well be right. All I can do is tangle. All I can say is:

You seem sad, but you're telling lies

Getting lost in the shuffle of alibis

Seasons change, so do you, so do I

Where do I go?

Look back on indiscretion, love

Reaction, I want action

No, no, no

Trying hard not to let you go (oh, so cold)

'Cause you just never let it show

There you go wandering along

People come and people go

Where do you go when you're not at home?

There is always more than meets the eye

Flew so fast, fell from the sky below

In the end, I'm happy in my galoshes. Happy stomping through the rainy mud of my childhood. Happy to remember the crazy chaos of a life dedicated to music and nearly destroyed by drugs. Happy to stop and put pencil to paper and, as best I can, mark my journey to this point.

I am back with Eric, Dean, and Robert, and that makes me happy. We have rededicated ourselves to our art and our fans. I am grateful that our musical base, built on integrity and a need to express a real kind of rock and roll, is still intact.

For all the success, our current tour hasn't been easy. I fell off the wagon. During the breaks, when I was able to spend time at home, I'd sit on my couch and not move for hours on end. For years I've known goddamn well that I'm a drunk, but who wants to admit that? After kicking the strong stuff, why couldn't I have a little drink now and then? What harm was there in a small indulgence? The answer was serious harm—potentially fatal harm. For me, putting a drink in my mouth is something like putting a lead blanket over my heart. There's been so much pain in the past few years that I'm afraid to feel, or commit. I pray that this will end. I don't want to be alone anymore. I want to be able to love again. The dream of every drunk—to be able to manage their drinking—is one that has died hard for me. My prayer is that, once and for all, that dream is good and dead.

So I'm back to counting days. It's nearly two months since I've had a drink. By the time you read this book, my hope is that it will be six months. I embrace the day-at-a-time mind-set. For me, there's no other way to live. I've got to stay present.

I am optimistic.

—————

I have to learn to see the beauty in the mundane. I believe this is a key to my spiritual well-being. I have to change my perception and see God's beauty in everything.

I believe what has kept me intriguing to the public while everyone is usually allowed their fifteen minutes of fame is my chameleon-like nature and my desire to break new sonic and musical ground. Having my own record label—Softdrive Records—has allowed me complete freedom to do just that.

Beyond music, I continue to paint and draw, even if everything ends up looking unconsciously like an Egon Schiele painting. All perspective is out the window.

I've realized a longtime dream by starting my own clothing line—Scott Weiland Collection by English Laundry. I love the creativity and artfulness behind great clothes.

Someone called me a jet-setter. Well, it's one thing to simply jet-set, but to do it while racing down the edge of a razor? Now that takes a certain kind of moxie and the constitution of a cockroach.

I have songs to write and songs to sing. I have ideas for drawings, movies, and other books. My goal is to stay inspired and inspire others. No matter how abstract or diverse my work, I want to leave a footprint of someone passionately interested in expressing his heart and soul. I'm still making that footprint.

I am not dead and not for sale.

THERE HAVE BEEN A LOT OF BANDS AND
MUSICIANS WE HAVE PLAYED WITH, OR WHO HAVE
INFLUENCED US, OR WHO IN SOME WAY HAVE
LEFT A LASTING IMPRESSION. SOME OF THESE ARE:

Neil Young

The Doors

Cheap Trick

Butthole Surfers

The Flaming Lips

Cage the Elephant

Sugartooth

Megadeth

Jane's Addiction

Red Hot Chili Peppers

Green Day

Elton John

Aerosmith

Thelonious Monster

Black Rebel Motorcycle Club

Linkin Park

Wiskey Biscuit

Ringo

The Rolling Stones

SELECTIONS
from my
SKETCHBOOK

CIRCUS
PEOPLE
DONT
JUDGE

As
osene
antic

ic-
pho-
honse
of the
er, warm

wi
wood
that line

ESOTER-
OS
VENTILATOR

VOX

DUMB
LOVE

theres
so much I
want to
teach you if
you only
have the
time.

theres so
much I could
teach you if
you only
have the
time...

century, and succeeding rulers expanded its holdings. In 1968.

t for
from
after

nstein
n Vi-
or-
ing
in
70

The Golden Carriage

I Don't Believe

I Don't Believe in Anythi...

I Don't Believe in me

I Don't Believe in love

I Don't Believe in Yo...

I Don't Believe in Anymo...

I Don't Believe in Peace

I Don't Believe in Hype

I (Don't) Believe All of i...

I (Don't Believe)

I Just Don't Believe

...The verses
Always come
when they're
called.
But I Don't
Call them.
Who Does?

Sky
is the
Only
Resurrection
For
Depression

WHY DID I introduce You to My WORLD?

I Love You to the Moon

Secret **Failure** Panel:

DONT FeeL
THE FADER
DONT Feel
the Heat
DonT Fee l
the FADeR
JUST eat
SHit
AND DR!

RACISM RACISM

RACISM IS AN IDEA OR PERSONAL BELIEF THAT ONE PARTICULAR
RACE IS SUPIOROR OVER ANOTHER BECAUSE OF VARIOUS REASONS
INCLUDING SKIN COLOR, RELIGIOS BELIEFS, PERSONAL EXPERIENCES
(WHICH DONT MEAN SHIT), AND EVEN STUPID NATIONALISTIC
ATTITUDES. ITS TIME WE DISMISSED ALL THIS HATRED TOWARDS
ONE ANOTHER AND TRY TO CREATE A BETTER WORLD FOR ALL OF US
TO LIVE IN SINCE WERE HERE TOGETHER WHETHER YOU LIKE IT OR
NOT. OTHER ISSUES SUCH AS NUCLEAR WAR, POLICE BRUTALITY
(ABUSIVE AUTHORITY), ANIMAL RIGHTS, AND WICKED EVIL BIASED
GOVERNMENTS(PROFITEERS) ARE FAR MORE OF IMPORTANT ISSUES
THAN WHAT A PERSON LOOKS LIKE. ALL RACISM HAPPENS TO BE
IS A PARTICULAR PERSON OR PEOPLE WHO HATE AND DETEST ANOTHER
PERSON OR PEOPLE BECAUSE OF THEY HAVE BEEN RAISED OR BRAIN
WASHED BY PROGRAMING PARENTS OR MISLEAD BY INSECURE SO CALLED
FRIENDS.TO BELIEVE THE OTHER IS INFERIOR, EVIL, OR JUST PLAIN
STUPID. AS FOR PERSONAL EXPERIENCES, MENTIONED EARLIER, OPEN
UP AND USE YOUR MEASLEY LITTLE FUCKING MIND AND REALISE THERE
IS A BAD APPLE IN EVERY GROUP AND YOU CANNOT BLAME AN ENTIRE
RACE FOR A FEW IDIOTS MISTAKES. FOR EVERY ONE IDIOT THERE ARE
MANY MORE CARING, PEACEFUL AND NICE PEOPLE. AND AS FOR
PRIDE IN YOUR RACE, I AINT PROUD, IM ASHAMED FOR WHAT WHITE
PEOPLE HAVE DONE TO BLACKS, JEWS, THE NATIVE AMERICAN INDIAN,
AND MANY OTHER PEOPLES IN THE PAST AND ARE CONTINUING TO DO
EVEN THIS VERY MINUTE. THESE ARE JUST OUR OPINIONS BUT VERY
STRONG BELIEFS AND WE WONT LET ANYONE TAKE THEM AWAY FROM
US BECAUSE YOU FUCKING CANT. YOU CAN KICK OUR ASSES A
MILLION TIMES BUT WE WILL KEEP PUSHING FOR EQUALITY. VIOLENCE IS
YOUR ANSWER NOT OURS. WE ARE PEACEFUL BUT WILL NOT BE PUSHED AROUND.

MEAT FACTS(DEAD ANIMAL)

WHATS IN MEAT? BESIDES LOTS OF SATURATED FATS AND CHOLESTEROL; CARCINOGENS, PESTICIDES
HORMONES AND ANTIBIOTICS TO PROMOTE ANIMALS ABNORMAL GROWTH AND FIGHT DISEASE CAUSED BY
OVER CROWDING. IS MEAT A HEALTH HAZARD? MEAT IS DIRECTLY LINKED TO HEART DISEASE
(AMERICANS #1 KILLER), HARDENING OF THE ARTERIES, HIGH BLOOD PRESSURE, CANCER OF THE COLON
AND BOWEL, KIDNEY AND LIVER DISEASE. ALSO BEING NOTHING MORE THAN ROTTING FLESH IT IS HIGHER
IN BACTERIA THAN IN ANY OTHER FOOD. WHAT ABOUT THE ANIMALS? THOSE NEAT LITTLE PLASTIC
PACKAGES IN THE MARKET USED TO HAVE LIVES OF THEER OWN. TODAYS INTENSIVE CONFINEMENT SYSTE
REDUCE ANIMALS TO "MEAT MACHINES". PIGS AND COWS ARE CASTRATED WITHOUT ANESTHESIA AND KEP
IN OVER CROWDED PENS, UNABLE TO TURN AROUND OR GROOM THEMSELVES. VEAL COWS ARE SEPERATED
THIER MOTHERS AT BIRTH, KEPT IN TOTAL DARKNESS AND DEPRIVED OF IRON. THREE BILLION CHICK
INTO SOUP OR POT PIES. PLEASE HELP US STOP THIS TORTURE. BOYCOTT MEAT . CONSIDER VEGTA

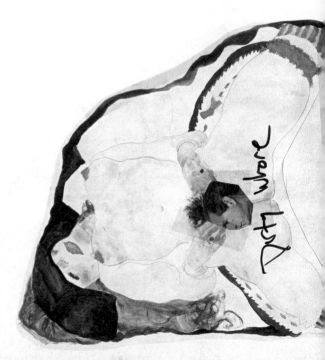

Dirty whore

gether,   rre said, What are
e back in again. And they said, 'No, no,
please. We've had six months of
this. It's been driving us
crazy. We want to
unplug all this stuff
and get back to
recording
normally. "

OOGES CBS

ger/Your Pretty
on/Raw Power/
Death Trip

ond, September 10
3 at Western
ed, May 1973
lid not chart
vocals),
Asheton
Bowie)
oducer:

N OF THE
1971, Iggy
nd mow lawns.
vkd Bowie
lim a deal with
f the album.
Stooges
f guitar
set that
flesh Rag, De
ommercial,
he only one
hoped into

Pilot
Weiland *Fuck off*
Crashes

Stone Temple Pilots
lead singer Scott Weiland
was awol from a court
ordered California drug
rehab center Thursday,
and a warrent was issued
for his arrest. The rock
band had to cancle it's
summer tour

By PETER YOON
Times Staff Writer

Kerri Walsh did
what to expect
ticed with Mi
time in al
thought
A
so

What

DISCREDIT THE BIBLE

IS DEAD!

UNITY AT ANY COST

ONE WORLD GOVERNMENT

ONE SUPER CHURCH

Singer Weiland faces jail time.

Rocker Weiland Skips Out Of Rehab

Officials said that Weiland was only
allowed to leave the house if accompanied
by a center supervisor, but he left without permission. The prior conviction
in 1995 for having illegal substances on
him had finally caught up with him.

By LAUREN PETERSON
Times Staff Writer

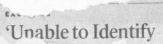

'Unable to Identify

BEAT!

AND

the BEST! BI

BRA!

UNABLE to IDENTIFY the Promises that were kept.
Your Prior convictions seem lost in lack of touch.
So I care. I should. I used to,
I do. to much it eats at my my
burning stomach. bile burns when there's
Lack of Food. God I Love you,
But Why Does it Have to Hurt. Lipstick,
Baptize me. Circumsize me. When I Dream
its of us Looking Down, Whatching
everyone else form the heavens. we can
Fly there, you freed me once. and should
me How to Fly. So Babn will you please
reTape my Wings.

PAIN MARKS

6910 Clinton St
La Ca 90036

INSPECTED
NO MONEY ENCLOSED
ENCLOSED: ☐ CASH
☐ MONEY ORDER
☐ CASHIER CHECK
AMOUNT
$ DEPOSITED TO YOUR ACCOUNT
DATE:

6158735
Scott Richard Weiland
Terminal Annex
P.O. Box 86164
La Ca 90086-0164

BRC#A1

33 USA

'Pattern of Abuse,'

NEIL YOUNG
TONIGHT'S THE NIGHT

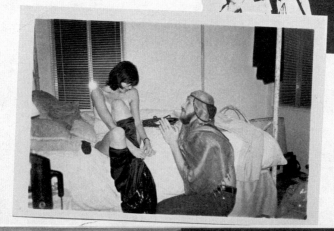

TOGETHER...

4158735
Scott Richard Weiland
Terminal Annex
P.O. Box 861147
La Ca 90086-1147

AUG 3 0 1998

6910 Clinton St
La Ca 90036

BRC / A1

Los Angeles Times

FRIDAY, JU

F RO

STP SINGER
BUSTED IN CAR

I Got You

But Its the Craving For
the Good life that
sees me thru troubled
  times.
WHEN MY MIND begins
to WANDer to
  the SPOON. AND

Ive Got You CAUSe
Your there to Bend
AND Nurture me
thru these troubled.
times. CAUSe the F.TX Begins
  to twist MY troubleD MiND

The Needle & the Damage Done

The Uncensored Story
of Scott Weiland
and Stone Temple Pilots

######

BY DAVID FRI...

PHOTOGRAPHS BY MARK SEL...

SINGER ARRESTED

But one day you're singing in the shower, something about "tangerine trees and marmalade skies," and you wonder what John Lennon was thinking. It's a shock to realize the Bard of Liverpool could also write dimwitted tripe.

Suddenly there's the creeping fear that your childhood adulation of Lennon, Kurt Cobain, Patti Smith — pick your deity — may have been misplaced. (And really, didn't you always suspect Led Zeppelin's fourth album was a slag-heap of blues rip-offs led by a prancing ninny who had supped too long at the well of J.R.R. Tolkien?)

Now you can pick up "Kill Your Idols" (Barricade Books, $16) and confirm your worst fears. This collection of essays, edited by Jim DeRogatis and Carmel Carrillo, demythologizes "classic" rock albums, including Bruce Springsteen's "Born to Run" ("slapped together by a gaggle of Ethel Merman wannabes," says David ...

DETHRONED: "Kill Your Idols" tears apart classics.

SINGER ARRESTED

"... Opaline," ... Capo,

Singer Arrested For Drug Possession

CRITIC'S NOTEBOOK

SUDDEN TRANSFORMATION: The former Opaline has become Café Coppa. For the most part, it's essentially a lower-priced version of the upscale Santa Monica restaurant Copa.

black velvet.

Every day it's something else. Soon celebrities will be arriving. And in the old restaurant in the old spot ...
... is on West Channel ... he's on ...

some of the best around. No can ... you go wrong, simple pastas en-... so formidable, ... for every vappoes filled with four ... There's something ... one in the main courses, the ob-... history shake and ...

Lawrence K. Ho / Lo...

(handwritten) FUCK All OF you fuckn merurus who Feed off of the Adrenilin of the Artists who they auk Do work why Do these Judges Kill those artIst opinio N?

(handwritten, left margin) MEAN WHILE NOTHING bAD the ... MORE than this times DOnt pAINt ...

ACKNOWLEDGMENTS

SCOTT WEILAND'S ACKNOWLEDGMENTS:

Deep gratitude to the people closest to me.

My kids, my inspiration and strength for staying on the road when
I feel like jumping on the first plane and coming home to them.

My parents, who have supported me beyond belief. Because of my
antics, they're still trying to catch up with their sleep.

My manager, Dana Dufine, who, from the inception of Velvet Revolver,
has become both a business partner and family friend.

My brother Michael and his wife, Michael. Michael was my best friend.
The legacy he left impacts me every day, and I could not have written
this book without his loving influence.

My musical partners. If you haven't worked in music, you can't imagine
the creative intimacy that flows between musicians. I am grateful
to every single musician I have encountered on stage and in the studio.

And to David Ritz, your quirkiness and knowledge is king, and your
patience with my rants and me goes beyond appreciation.

DAVID RITZ'S ACKNOWLEDGMENTS:

The brilliant Scott Weiland, Brant Rumble, Dana Dufine, Aubrey,
David Vigliano, Roberta, Alison, Jessica, Henry, Jim, Charlotte,
Nino, James, Isaac, Esther, Elizabeth, my nephews and nieces,
the Tuesday group, the great Pops Ritz, and pals Alan Eisenstock,
Herb Powell, and Harry Weinger. I am a believer.

Liv Sept 117